THE BEST OF Personal Excellence

The Magazine of Life Enrichment Volume 2

Executive Excellence Publishing
1344 East 1120 South
Provo, Utah 84606
phone: (801) 375-4060
fax: (801) 377-5960
e-mail: info@eep.com
web: http:\\www.eep.com

Ordering Information:
Individual Sales: Executive Excellence Publishing products are available through most bookstores. They can also be ordered directly from Executive Excellence at the address above.
Quantity Sales: Executive Excellence Publishing products are available at special quantity discounts when purchased in bulk by corporations, associations, libraries, and others, or for college textbook/course adoptions. Please write to the address above or call Executive Excellence Publishing Book Sales Division at 1-800-304-9782.
Orders for U.S. and Canadian trade bookstores and wholesalers: Executive Excellence Publishing books and audio tapes are available to the trade through LPC Group/Login Trade. Please contact LPC at 1436 West Randolph Street, Chicago, IL 60607, or call 1-800-626-4330.

First edition: 1999
Printed in the United States of America
10 9 8 7 6 5 4 3 2 1 03 02 01 00 99

ISBN: 1-890009-46-6

Also available on audio (two sets):
ISBN 1-890009-36-9 volume 3
ISBN 1-890009-51-2 volume 4

Cover design by Joe McGovern
Printed by Publishers Press

CONTENTS

Introduction

This book features some of the most popular articles to appear in the last two years of *Personal Excellence* magazine (1997–1998).

One Mission

Our mission is to promote personal and professional development based on constructive values, sound ethics, and timeless principles. This volume provides the best of theoretical concepts, practical experience, and applied knowledge—the triple play.

Five Sections

Please notice that we have organized material into five sections. The first section focuses on initiative and first steps toward success. The second section points to life direction—the image, picture or paradigm of an examined life. The third section suggests ways to overcome obstacles, move mountains, and balance your life. The fourth section promotes real progress in personal improvement and career development. And the final section urges ongoing growth, learning, and fitness.

Editorial Mix

We feel that the editorial mix of articles authored by political leaders, articulate executives, world-class athletes, and other peak performers makes magic. You will recognize many names, and some you may not recognize. These "no-names" are not nobodies. No one has a corner on the truth market. Indeed, the principles of effective life management and personal leadership are universal. So, of our authors, we require neither a Ph.D. nor a pedigree, but rather a conscience and moral apogee. We admit, without apology, that none of them is perfect, but we hope that all try to walk their talk.

Ken Shelton
Editor of *Personal Excellence*

SECTION 1

Taking Initiative

1

The Power of Choice

by M. Scott Peck

A *century ago,* the greatest dangers we faced arose from agents outside ourselves: microbes, flood and famine, and wolves in the forest at night. Today the greatest dangers—war, pollution, starvation—have their source in our own motives and sentiments: greed and hostility, carelessness and arrogance, narcissism and nationalism.

The study of values might once have been a matter of individual concern and deliberation as to how best to lead the "good life." Today it is a matter of collective survival. If we identify the study of values as a branch of philosophy, then it's time for all women and men to become philosophers—or else.

What do theologians mean when they say that we are "created in the image of God"? I believe that we have been given free will, the extraordinary power of choice. But the power to choose is the power to choose the bad or the good—to be loving or unscrupulously self-centered. What is the nature of this power? What motivates our choices?

Many people of different races, cultures, and nationalities are strongly motivated by money. Indeed, it would be quite safe to refer to the human species as *Homo economicus.* But economically motivated acts are not necessarily good acts. Often they are obviously malicious and sometimes downright murderous. If we cannot routinely learn to submit the personal profit motive, when appropriate, to higher principles, then in all likelihood—and quite quickly—we will murder ourselves off. Such higher principles are matters of values or ethics. To be truly Homo sapiens, wise enough to figure out how to survive, then it will not be enough for us to remain merely *Homo economicus;* we must somehow become *Homo ethicus.*

We have profoundly different cognitive lenses through which we view the world, and hence profoundly different styles of thinking by which we make our value judgments, our ethical decisions. Ethical behavior is, of necessity, conscious behavior. If we are unconscious of our motives, it is unlikely that we will behave in a consistently ethical manner. If we are not aware of the particular lens through which we view the world, we do not have true choice about what we see and how we respond.

We not only have our own lenses, but a range of different lenses. There are two results. One is to make it possible for us to question the validity of our perceptions and values. The capacity for ethical behavior is dependent on the capacity for such self-questioning. Virtually all evil is committed by people who are absolutely certain they know what they are doing.

The other result is that it enables us to make multidimensional decisions. If we think just logically or just emotionally or just intuitively, then our decisions will be only logical or only intuitive or only emotional. But if we become aware of different cognitive styles, it opens up the possibility for us to make decisions that are emotional, logical, and intuitive. We can then integrate different ways of knowing; to think, and to speak, with both our right brains and our left brains.

I believe such integration to be essential to our collective salvation. Integrity is derived from the ability to integrate. If we are going to think and behave with full integrity, we must learn how to integrate our different ways of perceiving the world so as to develop a multidimensional, integrated world view. To behave ethically is to behave with integrity. In raising our consciousness of the different styles by which we make our value judgments, we are pointed toward greater wholeness and integrity.

M. Scott Peck is a psychiatrist, diagnostician, consultant, best-selling author, and a founder of The Foundation for Community Encouragement.

2

Decide to Decide

by J. W. "Bill" Marriott, Jr.

Early in life, I learned an important lesson, "deciding to decide." For me, it meant that as a young man I simply would not do certain things like being unfaithful, smoking, drinking alcohol, or using drugs. I chose to put my family first, then my church, then my business. And I decided that that would be the last time I'd make a decision about those temptations or priorities.

Like changing lifelong bad habits to prevent a heart attack, deciding to decide has ramifications that go beyond work to profoundly affect health, home, and family. Thomas Carlyle once said: "A man lives by believing something, not by debating many things." Once you decide to decide, life becomes surprisingly simple. You don't have to think about certain issues or questions again. You simply get on with things and don't waste time and energy debating and arguing problems and possibilities.

When you decide to decide, you're not starting from scratch each time you're faced with an issue. You've got your answer already.

Deciding to make family a top priority, for example, can be very gratifying. My happiest moments are those spent with my wife, Donna, our children and grandchildren. We view the family as the central source of daily support in good times and bad. We laugh together, pray together, and give each other a boost when we're down.

There is satisfaction to be had in standing firm against the temptations that come with contemporary life. Saying no consistently can give a sense of real power in a world that often seems out of control.

When I suffered my heart attack, I learned that robbing Peter to pay Paul has dangerous consequences. I stole my health to satisfy my workaholic habits.

Deciding to decide is nothing more than recognizing and accepting that there's only so much you can do or handle intelligently. Not everyone finds the idea of hard-and-fast choices easy to accept, but I find it liberating. It also keeps me humble by reminding me that no one's judgment is so infallible that signposts and rules aren't necessary.

Each of us faces a common challenge: achieving balance. No one is likely to find the perfect balance. But in searching for it, you might discover talents you didn't know you possessed, strength you never imagined, and a dream worth spending a lifetime to build.

J. W. "Bill" Marriott, Jr., is chairman and CEO of Marriott International.

3

Let the Magic Begin

by Cathy Lee Crosby

A*s I reflect* on my life, what amazes me most are the wondrous gifts I receive from incredibly difficult times. I once lost everything that I'd worked my entire life to achieve, everything I thought mattered; and yet, I regained my connection with who I am. It's almost as if the "wounding" was sacred in its ability to reconnect me with the Divine purpose of my life.

Deepak Chopra has said, "Only the heart knows the correct answer. It taps into the cosmic computer and takes everything into account. The heart has a computing ability that is far more accurate and precise than anything within the limits of rational thought." The heart opens the door to a whole new world of possibility. "You need chaos in your soul to give birth to a dancing star," wrote Nietzsche.

The Bliss Zone

You can regain your sense of awe and wonder, regain your ability to create life from the core of your heart, and re-enter the realm of pure possibility by living moment to moment in the Bliss Zone.

Personally, I feel it's a very exciting time to live. Dissatisfaction, alienation, frustration, aggression, and battling to survive are no longer acceptable definitions of life to us. We know that there is a better way to live, but often we keep this thought to ourselves, because we are not sure what to do about it. We also know that we have gone outside of ourselves as far as we can possibly go, searching for answers to living successful, yet meaningful, creative and connected lives. Now we have come to the conclusion that there is no other direction to go but inside ourselves.

Having taken the journey, I have come to understand that life is a circle in which we all play a unique part. I've learned firsthand that this circle consists of the Divine energizing each of us, and each one of us, in return, utilizing this dynamic, creative force to glorify, re-ignite and reconnect with the Whole. Without this circle, chaos reigns. Life becomes out of balance, and so do we. Our lives become a struggle to survive in a game of dog-eat-dog, might makes right, and I win—you lose.

Unintentionally and unconsciously, I did just that; and what it cost me, financially, emotionally, and psychologically, was immense. I fell through the trapdoor with a resounding thud.

At the same time, however, I was blessed in a way I never could have imagined. I was given the "opportunity" of learning to see with more than my eyes; to hear with more than my ears; and to feel with more than my hands. I was given the chance to experience a veritable treasure chest of wonder: the veil of illusion, the peace of "nothingness," the power of dreams, the playground of coincidences, the natural rhythm of the universe, the vibrancy of being free from the chains of my past, the comfort of a reconnected family bond, the pure innocence of living from the core of my heart.

There is still so much more to experience, so much more to learn, and so much more to unfold. But the foundation of who I am is now cast in gold, and eternally fired by a direct connection to my heart. Struggling for answers, and trying to use my will alone to demand "my place in the world," has been erased from the blackboard of my experience. In the long run, my efforts in that regard proved fruitless and empty.

There is peace and security in knowing that you have been put on this earth for a very special purpose, that you are no longer alone, and that you are connected to everything that ever was and ever will be. It's an absence of the consideration of time, boundaries, and fear. The energy from the universe gives you "life," and that energy is re-ignited in you when you live in the Bliss Zone.

Magical Places

I believe that we are all born into this magical place, but unfortunately, are never taught how to live within its realm. So, when our world becomes filled with challenges, heartbreak, and loss, we unwittingly disconnect from our natural core. We unconsciously go out of the Bliss Zone and into "reality" in an effort to overcome our adverse circumstances. At that precise moment, whenever it occurs, our world of innocence, joy, awe, and wonder comes crashing headlong into what we now believe is the "real world." This propels us further away from our true source of power, creativity, and wisdom.

We often believe that we are what we "do" in life, and that our joy comes from the results we achieve. But that's only part of the story. To experience the full richness, depth, and magic in every moment, whether we are actually "achieving" anything or not, we must learn how to flow from the pure inner essence of who we are. This allows us to connect with the essence of everything, so we can join in the "dance," always open to the infinite possibilities existing within its natural rhythm.

Cathy Lee Crosby is owner of her own production company, CLC Productions, and author of *Let the Magic Begin.*

4

Living Consciously

An interview with Nathaniel Branden

What do you mean by living consciously?

Living consciously means being present to what we are doing while we are doing it. It means being eager to acquire information, knowledge, and feedback on our interests, values, goals, purposes, and projects. It means having self-awareness through self-examination. No one can be said to be operating consciously when self-awareness and self-examination are not being tended.

Why do many people live unconsciously?

For a variety of reasons. One is inertia. Operating consciously requires work. We do not like to confront fears, because we may not always like what we see. Or it may involve bringing the searchlight of consciousness to bear on our lives and having to confront and deal with unresolved pain. Or again we may have certain wishes or desires that are irrational, and we close our eyes to that fact so we can pursue them, whereas if we were to operate consciously we would be stopped in our tracks by the awareness of how self-destructive these desires could be.

What are outcomes of living unconsciously?

Well, people date, marry, raise their children, and work semi-unconsciously. It's not surprising that the results they produce in their lives are not gratifying. The less conscious we are, the more we operate mechanically, and consequently the more restricted our options are in any situation; therefore, we are less effective. We may choose to ignore clear indicators that our strategies and tactics have become obsolete. But rather than change our strategies or tactics and adapt to the marketplace, we close our eyes and keep telling ourselves, "Well, this used to work."

What are outcomes of living consciously?

The more conscious we are, the more options we see; therefore, the more effective and powerful we can be in responding to life's challenges. When asked to explain the transformation at General Electric, Jack Welch said, "Confidence, candor, and a willingness to look at reality when it is painful." This goes to the very heart of living consciously.

On a personal level, let's consider love and marriage. Conscious people do not wait until they are married several years to find out who they have selected. They pay attention from the beginning, and when they see signs of danger or signs that the relationship is a big mistake, they stop. Unconscious people ignore signs that a mistake is being made until they are in much worse trouble. People who operate consciously know how their behavior affects their partner and how their partner's behavior affects them. They are more tuned into the dynamics of the relationship.

What is the connection between consciousness and spirituality?

Spirituality pertains to consciousness when you are working on improving the quality of the relationship between your consciousness and reality; that is a spiritual pursuit. Many people consider themselves spiritual, but when it comes to how they actually live and conduct themselves, they are utterly unconscious.

Why is living consciously the responsible choice?

Our mind is our basic means of survival and adaptation to reality. If I want to work effectively, I had better see reality as clearly as I can. To ask why consciousness is important is like asking why sight is important. If I go through reality, if I move through the world figuratively speaking, with my eyes closed, I have good reason to be anxious.

And will that anxiety affect your esteem and relationships?

Yes, anxiety will negatively affect your relationships and your effectiveness in coping with life. By self-esteem, I mean the experience of being confident to cope with the basic challenges of life and to be worthy of happiness. How can I feel confident to cope with the challenges of life if I move through life either mechanically or mindlessly, or without giving thought to the consequences of my actions?

Why do otherwise intelligent people often act in a semi-conscious state?

I often conduct an exercise to help people learn how to operate more consciously and release the talents and abilities of the people they manage or lead. First, I ask them to identify what they want from the people they report to but rarely get. Then they devise a second list of what the people who report to them need but rarely get. Looking at the two lists side-by-side causes a great awakening. This exercise raises the level of consciousness of people who are very aware of what they need but don't get, but are too often oblivious to what the people who report to them need to get.

What can help a person stay in this state of high consciousness?

Be aware of the issue, and be aware of its importance. Also, be aware of the consequences of the choices you make. Look for areas where the problems, frustrations, and pains are, because those may be the areas where you have to upgrade your consciousness.

At the end of your book, you say, "Hey, your life is important. Honor and fight for your highest potential." Why leave readers with that message?

Because it is one of the things that should have been told them as children. For me it is one of the very most important things for anyone to understand. People resign themselves to frustrations much too regularly. They often give up on their own lives much too readily, much too easily.

Is that because they make a mistake and figure all is lost?

They are too quick to draw very malevolent and drastic conclusions from one or two disappointments or failures.

Nathaniel Branden is the author of *The Art of Living Consciously* and *The Six Pillars of Self-Esteem.*

5

Time Trials

by John Cleese

As a harried person for whom time itself is precious, you regularly confront the grim reality that there are only 24 hours in a day. You could, of course, change that situation by unilaterally adopting the 48-minute hour, gaining six hours a day.

Declaring a 30-hour day for yourself poses insurmountable problems, though. You'd show up for the 7 a.m. train 84 minutes early and miss the 4 p.m. staff meeting by an hour.

As an alternative, you can use the available 24 hours more effectively. This requires organizing your time, a Holy Grail that has probably inspired more published verbiage than the Savior's own sacred goblet. However, since most people never find time to read the weighty tomes filled with timesaving advice, I'll provide a few brief guidelines here.

The first step in becoming organized is listing your tasks. Don't worry about getting them down in any order: just brainstorm them onto the page.

Next categorize each task under one of two headings: the positive active tasks and the reactive tasks. Positive active tasks are those you must do to achieve the larger objectives in your job. Reactive tasks are all the junk that lands on your desk every day and has to be dealt with to keep things running.

Now determine how important each task is, and how urgent it is. Importance and urgency are not the same thing at all. A relatively trivial task may be quite urgent because it entails a rapidly approaching deadline. On the other hand, you may never get to a very important task because its effects are far-reaching but not immediate.

Your goal in creating a schedule is to allocate as much time as possible to the active, important matters and deal as efficiently as possible with urgent, relatively trivial reactive tasks. This often involves setting aside a regular, limited time for handling quick, pressing business—preparing a weekly report, for instance, or dictating correspondence—rather than sprinkling these unavoidable but distracting jobs throughout your business day.

Allow yourself blocks of uninterrupted time for the important tasks. You will need to be ruthless in guarding this chronological treasure. Have your phone calls answered and messages taken. Post a slavering, bloodthirsty Doberman at your closed office door or, if you really want to be intimidating, a well-trained secretary with strict orders that you are not to be disturbed. If your open-door policy has become so entrenched that you simply can't turn people away from your office, then take some time to work elsewhere—a spare conference room, perhaps, or even at home.

Becoming organized is actually a two-stage process. First prioritize and schedule the tasks for which you are responsible. When you have this schedule firmly in hand, you can move on to the next stage: delegating some of these tasks and freeing more time for the active, important tasks on your agenda.

But a discussion of delegating work will have to wait for another month. It's nearly 15 o'clock, and the Chinese food delivery is due any moment now.

John Cleese is co-founder of Video Arts, a leading producer of business training videos.

6

Castles and Cobwebs

by Norman R. Augustine

R*eality matters*—even in this age of virtual reality, stealth and artificial intelligence. Reality is not to be found in the offices of the takeover artists, the deal-makers or the arbitrageurs. Reality is not in the offices of the executives, accountants or the lawyers. I believe that "where it's at," and where it will be in the critical years ahead, is all those places where individuals reside who perform work directly related to producing a useful, quality product or providing an essential service efficiently and effectively—and ethically as well. Or where people are nurturing an important innovation. That is "where it's at"—despite all the protestations to the contrary.

In most areas of human endeavor, the relationship between the fraction of contributors and the fraction of their contribution is both highly predictable and highly concentrated. For a whole range of human activities, a small fraction of participants produce a large fraction of the accomplishments. As Robert Frost noted, the world is full of willing people—"some willing to work, and the rest willing to let them."

Being a contributor means working in risk-filled environments. But neither a company, a country, nor an individual can prosper and grow by dreaming dreams that bear no risk. We must practice due prudence, we must embody reasonable caution, and we must not court danger thoughtlessly. But prudent risk is an essential and significant component of progress.

As Thoreau once said: "If you have built castles in the air, that is where they should be. Now put the foundations under them."

According to legend, the 14th century Scottish king, Robert the Bruce, was once hiding out from English pursuers on a remote island. Defeated and dejected, he noticed a spider trying painfully to fix its web to a wooden beam. Again and again the spider tried, only to fail each time. But it wouldn't quit. And in the end, it succeeded. His spirit restored, Robert the Bruce gathered a small band of followers and, against great odds, drove the English out of Scotland.

Consider these examples: Sam Walton tried and failed for years to get the company he worked for to open a discount home supply store—then he went out on his own. English novelist John Creasey got 753 rejection slips before he published 564 books. Babe Ruth struck out 1,330 times, but also hit 714 home runs.

Then there's the story told of the fellow who dropped out of grade school, ran a country store, went broke, took 15 years to pay off his debts, had an unhappy marriage, ran for the Senate and lost twice, delivered a speech that became a classic but the audience was indifferent. He was attacked daily by the press and despised by half the country. He signed his name, you will recall, "A. Lincoln."

Take Part

Life is not a spectator sport. This is not the beginning of a trial run. Your world needs you. Don't climb up into the world's grandstand—there are too many spectators there already. If you think the schools need improvement, join the PTA and improve them. Better yet, take up teaching. Give your job your best if you think it deserves it. But, if not, get another job—or start your own business and run it your way.

Whatever the future may hold, whether it be putting foundations under castles in the clouds or fixing cobwebs to beams just a little too far away, I am confident that you will do yourself proud.

Norman R. Augustine is chairman and CEO of Lockheed Martin Corporation.

7

Transcending Mediocrity

by Kevin Freiberg

I*n a do-more-with-less world,* it is still possible to go home at the end of the day emotionally charged. The following principles will help you develop the courage, confidence, and contagious enthusiasm that are characteristic of an extraordinary life.

1. Find a purpose you're crazy about. The ability to exercise strong leadership requires inner strength and high self-esteem. Inner strength and high self-esteem follow from having a strong sense of purpose and direction. There are no heights to which the human spirit can't rise when we passionately believe that our lives are wrapped up in a cause that gives us a sense of meaning and significance. When we see how our individual efforts contribute to a larger cause or a worthy purpose we fulfill one of our deepest desires—the desire to make a difference. When we know that our lives and our work have meaning, we still have energy at the end of the day because the sanctity of labor has been affirmed. Find a purpose you're crazy about, a purpose to which you are willing to give the totality of who you are, and who knows—you may recapture your idealism in a world that often gives little reason for being idealistic. You may even find a purpose so captivating that it awakens the collective energies of the people with whom you work and inspires them to soar.

2. Make your life and work an adventure. People who live above the level of mediocrity are adventurous and playful. They work at turning routine into festivity. They get more out of life because they expect more out of life. So, decide today to become more curious, interested, and inquisitive. Take the time to rediscover the people you know. If you've been sleepwalking through life, wake up and start seeking new challenges. Make every moment count by giving yourself permission to work with fewer inhibitions and live just a little bit more adventurously. What have you got to lose? If you work in a company that doesn't seem to tolerate nuts, maybe it's time to lead by example and start a revolution in the part of the organization that you control or influence. If you've been there and done that, maybe it's time to muster the courage to leave. Life is too short and we work too much of it to be emotionally and spiritually dead.

3. Don't take yourself too seriously. There is a spirit of liberty among people who don't take themselves too seriously. When we loosen up, we are more open to new ideas and less resistant to constructive feedback. When we are wrapped up in protecting our egos and holding on to life too tightly, we become rigid, defensive, and boring. Think about the people you have the most fun being around. Are they people who can make you laugh by making light of their idiosyncrasies? Do yourself a big favor—lighten up. Your loved ones, your employees, and your customers will appreciate you for creating an environment where they can have fun.

4. Dare to dream. Dreams stimulate our senses and awaken our entrepreneurial spirit. They fuel our imagination, release our creative energy, and draw forth a deep sense of commitment to action. It's difficult to take action toward something you can't envision. It's almost impossible to envision something you don't have the freedom to dream about. People who lose their dreams have nothing to hope for, nothing to live for. Dreams help us experience the richness of life. There will always be those who respond to your dreams by saying, "You gotta be kidding! Are you nuts?" Albert Einstein once said, "Great spirits always encounter violent opposition from mediocre minds." The most significant achievements begin in the minds of those who have the courage to follow their dreams.

5. Dare to be different. Make room for the untried, the unpredictable, and the unexpected. When people who think differently hit you with a fresh idea that makes sense, go for it! If it bombs, learn from it. If it works, celebrate like crazy. But remember to keep looking for the new, the unconventional, and the unfamiliar way of doing things. The payoffs can be immense.

*6. **Take intelligent risks.*** Daring to be unconventional certainly has its risks. But risk is an integral part of learning anything new. Think of the first time you learned to do something you thoroughly enjoy. Whether it was learning to ski, swim, play an instrument, or fly an airplane, it required that you take a risk. If you had not assumed the risk, you wouldn't be living life as fully. There will always be those who lounge in the safety of convention, who criticize you for daring to live on the edge. Growing, getting better, and experiencing freedom, fullness, and vitality begins with a willingness to step outside our comfort zones.

*7. **Never stop learning.*** In a rapidly changing environment, the world takes no pity on the person who gets lazy about learning. Some marriages grow stale because the vitality created by each partner bringing something new and exciting back into the relationship ceases to exist. Don't assume you can rely on yesterday's strategies to create tomorrow's success.

Transcending mediocrity involves retooling, reeducating, and reinventing ourselves so that we continually add value. Examine each of your life dimensions and ask yourself, "What have I learned lately that will cause one or more of these areas to grow? What have I learned recently that will add value to and enrich the lives of the people with whom I live and work?"

Life is a choice! The choices we make will determine the content of our character, the quality of our lives, and the performance of our organizations. By choosing to transcend mediocrity, we become people who experience freedom, fullness, and vitality in life.

Kevin Freiberg is co-author of the national bestseller, *NUTS! Southwest Airlines' Crazy Recipe for Business and Personal Success.*

8

Energy Over Ego

by Ken Blanchard

W*e can't control* a lot of events in life. Bad things will happen. About all we can control in life is how we respond to those events. We can always choose to control our response.

Tom Crum, author of *The Magic of Conflict* and an aikido expert, taught me that in aikido, a form of self-defense, if someone tries to punch you, you don't try to block the punch, but rather you use the energy from the punch to your own advantage. When you try to block a punch, you are using your power and strength to resist the other person's power and strength. This sets up a win-lose confrontation.

In aikido, your strategy is to step aside with an accepting and pivoting movement, using the attacker's energy to throw him or to apply a neutralizing technique. The key, as Tom teaches it, is to learn how to be centered, with both mind and body relaxed and alert. In this state of heightened awareness and connectedness, you stop thinking about mechanics and go with the flow of energy.

One key concept that Tom teaches is centering. In skiing, as well as in life, people do fine when everything is going well, but when they hit a bump, they tend to focus their attention and energy on the bump. As a result, they very often end up falling.

Tom teaches you to center yourself if you hit a bump. Centering means gathering all of your energy and focusing it on your physical center. For example, if you stand next to someone and put your hand gently on his chest and push, you can easily move him. But if he focuses his energy on his center and concentrates there, you can't move him with the same energy you applied before. He will stand firm, without straining.

When you are centered, you are connected to a universal energy. You use adversities as opportunities to learn, grow, and move forward in your life. If you respond to events in a centered way, you remain positive and progressive. You keep your energy and perspective positive and focused on your learning and goals. If you are not centered, you are easily knocked off balance in tough times. You negatively respond to everything that happens, and you tend to take adversity personally.

Boost Self-Esteem

I teach the importance of self-esteem in my leadership seminars because it's clear to me that managers today must be more effective as coaches, counselors and cheerleaders, rather than as judges, critics, and evaluators.

But I realize that it is almost impossible for people who don't feel good about themselves to play these new roles. I began to see that effective leadership begins on the inside and moves out. After all, only people who genuinely like themselves can build the self-esteem of others without feeling that it takes something away from them.

I began to sense that perhaps the quickest and most powerful way to enhance our self-esteem and make ourselves more loving is a spiritual awakening. I say "awakening" because I believe that all of us develop amnesia after we are born. We forget where we came from.

We get ourselves into trouble when we believe there is nothing more powerful, knowledgeable, and loving than ourselves. I think the most widespread addiction in the world is the human ego. Ego stands for *Edging God Out.*

In my book, *We Are the Beloved,* I try to assist people with what I call the HELP model.

H stands for humility. In *The Power of Ethical Management,* Norman Vincent Peale and I said, "People with humility don't think less of themselves, they just think of themselves less." In other words, it's healthy to feel good about yourself, but don't get carried away. Humility reminds you that there is someone more powerful, more loving, and more caring than you. I guarantee that getting in touch with your own vulnerability and centering on a greater power will make you a better person.

E stands for excellence. Most people think of excellence as being the best—better than anyone else. Unfortunately, there can only be one Number One. To think of excellence in this manner sets up life as a win-lose proposition, where the only person that matters to you is good old Number One. The excellence that helps keep you on course is available to everyone. It is the process of rising up and becoming the very best you that you can be. This means balancing between achieving results and maintaining important relationships.

L stands for listening. One of my favorite teachers used to say, "If God had wanted us to talk more than listen, He would have given us one ear and two mouths." One reason we have trouble staying out of our own way is that we don't take time to quiet ourselves and get centered. When fog settles in over the seaport, ships listen for the foghorn to know where the dangers are. The sound of the horn helps them stay on course. We, too, need to listen so that we don't stray off course. The old habit of charging hard through life leaves little time for listening to that voice that calls us to a more excellent way of living.

P stands for praising. Of all the concepts I have taught people over the years, the most important has been the power of praising. The key to developing people is to catch them doing something right, so you can pat them on the back and recognize their performance. Nothing motivates people more than being caught in the act of doing something right. If you are to stay on course in your walk through life, you need to catch yourself doing things right as well.

If we take and accept the love that is there for us, we can be so much better at caring for, listening to and helping others as well as ourselves.

Ken Blanchard, co-author of *The One Minute Manager* series, is chairman of Blanchard Training and Development.

9

Manifest Your Destiny

by Wayne Dyer

Learning to love and trust can be difficult. It will be an exercise in futility if you rely upon your mind. When turned toward spiritual matters, the mind tries to come up with answers by using proofs, logic, and reasoning. It demands assurances.

The heart, focused on spiritual understanding, intuitively recognizes the value of love. Whereas the mind attempts to know the spirit by setting up conditions that must be met for there to be a release of love, the heart employs intuitive love as its way. It is not a conclusion of reasoning. It is the way of spontaneity, not the result of bargaining. The heart trusts the inner wisdom that it feels and knows, whereas the mind demands evidence before it will trust.

Authentic trust is only available through the knowing heart. When you enter this trusting space, everything will come to you that belongs to you because you have created the inner capacity to receive it. The search for happiness outside ourselves rekindles an idea that we are not whole and relegates prayer to the status of a plea to a boss or to God. We are then asking for favors rather than seeking a manifestation of our highest, inspired selves.

Prayer, at the highest spiritual level, is not asking for something to show up in your life. Authentic prayer is inviting divine desire to express itself through you for your highest purpose and good, and for the greater benefit of all. Prayer at this level expresses your oneness with divine energy.

The highest self wants you to experience peace or enlightenment. I define enlightenment as being immersed in and surrounded by peace. The more you trust in the wisdom that creates all, the more you will trust yourself. The result of trusting is that an enormous sense of peace becomes available to you. When the ego insists on winning, comparing or judging, you can soothe and calm the ego's fears with the peacefulness born of trust.

As this awareness grows, you will discover that you are a more peaceful person, and that enlightenment becomes the way of your life. Being independent of the good opinion of others and being detached from the need to be right are two powerful indicators that your life is shifting toward trust in yourself and trust in God. Still, many people in your life may disturb your peace. Then, the question is how to handle those people.

The people in our lives with whom we agree and share interests are easy to accept, but they teach us very little. Those who push our buttons and send us into a rage at the slightest provocation are our real teachers.

Give thanks for those great spiritual masters who have arrived in your life in the form of your children, current or former spouses, irritating neighbors, co-workers, and obnoxious strangers, for they help you stay in an enlightened, peaceful state. They let you know how much more work you have to do and in what ways you have not mastered yourself.

Peace occurs when your highest self is dominant. When you feel peace as the result of trust, you enjoy a healthy soul. When you trust, you know. And a knowing cannot be silenced by the contrary opinions of anyone you encounter. You will be independent of the good opinion of others when this trust becomes your way of life. You will not need to prove yourself to anyone, or to convince anyone of the rightness of your views.

You will be a silent sage, moving through this material plane with a knowing that you have tapped into a source of inspiration that provides you with all the sustenance you need.

Wayne Dyer is the author of 11 books, including *Manifest Your Destiny,* and has a doctorate in counseling psychology.

10

Long Walk to Freedom

by Nelson Mandela

I was not born with a hunger to be free. I was born free—free to run in the fields near my mother's hut, free to swim in the clear stream that ran through my village, free to ride the broad backs of slow-moving bulls. As long as I obeyed my father and abided by the customs of my tribe, I was not troubled by the laws of man or God.

It was only when I learned as a young man that my boyhood freedom was an illusion, that my freedom had already been taken from me, that I began to hunger for it.

The desire for freedom to live with dignity and self-respect has animated my life. It transformed a frightened man into a bold one, drove a law-abiding attorney to become a criminal, turned a family-loving husband into a man without a home, and forced a life-loving man to live like a monk.

I am no more virtuous or self-sacrificing than the next man, but I found that I could not even enjoy the poor and limited freedoms I was allowed when I knew my people were not free. The chains on any one of my people were chains on all of them; the chains on them were chains on me.

In that way, my commitment to my people, to the millions of South Africans I would never know or meet, was at the expense of the people I knew best and loved most. It was as simple and yet as incomprehensible as the moment a small child asks her father, "Why can't you be with us?" And the father must say the terrible words: "There are other children like you, a great many of them . . . "

During those long and lonely years, my hunger for the freedom of my own people became a hunger for the freedom of all people. The oppressor must be liberated just as surely as the oppressed. A man who takes away another's freedom is a prisoner of hatred; he is locked behind the bars of prejudice and narrow-mindedness. The oppressed and the oppressor alike are robbed of their humanity.

When I walked out of prison, my mission was to liberate the oppressed and the oppressor both. Some say that has now been achieved. But we are not yet free; we have merely achieved the freedom to be free, the right not to be oppressed. To be free is not merely to cast off one's chains, but to live in a way that respects and enhances the freedom of others.

The policy of apartheid created a deep wound in my country, but the decades of oppression and brutality produced men of such extraordinary courage, wisdom, and generosity that their like may never be known again. Perhaps it requires depth of oppression to create heights of character. My country is rich in the minerals and gems that lie beneath its soil, but I know that its greatest wealth is its people, finer than the purest diamonds.

I always knew that deep down in every human heart, there is mercy and generosity. No one is born hating another person. People must learn to hate, and if they can learn to hate, they can be taught to love, for love comes more naturally to the human heart. Man's goodness is a flame that can be hidden but never extinguished.

I have walked that long road to freedom. I have made missteps along the way, but I have discovered the secret after climbing a great hill: One only finds that there are many more hills to climb. I have taken a moment here to rest, to steal a view of the glorious vista that surrounds me, to look back on the distance I have come. But I can rest only for a moment, for with freedom comes responsibilities, and I dare not linger, for my long walk is not ended.

Nelson Mandela is president of the Republic of South Africa, and the author of *Long Walk to Freedom* from which this article is adapted by permission of Little, Brown and Co.

SECTION 2

Defining Direction

11

Create a New You

by Robert H. Schuller

P***lease, let me*** ask you some personal questions.

Who are you? What do you really believe? Is there anything or anyone you'd die for? Where are you coming from? What memories do you have? What pressures from the past may still drive you? Where are you headed? Does your life have direction? Purpose? Ambition? Passion? How rich—or poor—are you? What do you own? What do you owe? To whom? Are you satisfied? Should you be? What do you value? Are your friends good for you? Where have you chosen to live? Or did you choose? Are you a product of destiny or a person of decision? How are your relationships? What are your hopes and your hurts? Do they control you? What are your successes? Achievements? Dreams? Prayers? When, where, and how have you made a positive difference? What are your failures? When and why did you miss the mark? Any regrets? What's your greatest problem? Some person? Your position? Or, are you your biggest problem? Are you living with decisions you've made or failed to make? What decisive changes could you make? Are you in touch with your emotions? What would move you to tears? Are you in a rut? Do you dare to face the possibility of foreign feelings? Do you have dreams still unfulfilled? What persons, projects, passions, and performance would you pursue if you knew you wouldn't fail? What good and glorious impossibilities would you go after if you could see them as eventual achievements?

So, Now What?

So now—what do you want before your curtain drops? Wake up! A new dream will emerge from the shadows of yesterday and today to become a beautiful, bright light on your tomorrows!

Be open and receptive to a new vision—a new you, a new life, a beautiful, bright tomorrow. If you can dream it, you can do it! Here's how you'll make it happen. Start here and now, by asking yourself: "Will you make it simple and make it work?" You then respond, "Yes, I accept the challenge."

From all of the positive people I've met, all the books I've written and read, I can sum up the eight principles of powerful thinking in eight rhyming lines:

Possibilities must be weighted.
Priorities must be swayed.
Plans must be laid.
Commitments must be made.
The price must be paid.
The timing may be delayed.
The course must be stayed.
And the trumpets will be played.

I'm often asked, "Dr. Schuller, what is the most helpful book that you've ever written?" I usually answer, "My last one." But if you ask me today, I have a new answer: "My next one."

I don't want you to fail. I want you to succeed as you never have before! Simply believe, "If it's going to be, it's up to me!"

The 21st Century will belong to people who possess a strong, sensitive, spiritual individualism. So, move up and get ahead with the power of possibility thinking.

Only one person on earth can dream your dreams—you! Only one person can decide to make your dreams come true—you! Decide not to be a product, a computer, or a puppet—but a person! "If it's going to be, it's up to me."

Robert H. Schuller is the best-selling author of many books, including *If It's Going To Be It's Up To Me*. He is also founder of The Crystal Cathedral.

12

You Are Special

by Fred Rogers

Over the years, I've had some extraordinary teachers who have helped me learn about life. One teacher was my grandfather, Fred Brooks McFeely. He wasn't a teacher by training, but he taught me through his love. Because he cared so much about me, I wanted to learn from him. I can still remember his saying to me, "Freddy, I like you, just the way you are." That meant so much to me.

Communication for me has always been more than words. When I was five, I found I could easily express my feelings through my fingers at the piano. And as an adult I find writing the melodies and the lyrics for our Neighborhood program has been an important way for me to express a wide range of emotions.

To deepen what I could bring to television, I added seminary to my studies for eight years during my lunch hours and evenings. At my ordination as a minister, I was given a special charge to serve children and their families through the mass media.

I care deeply about communication, about words—what we say and what we hear. While television communication might look simple to some, it isn't. Children are not simple; neither are adults. I have always given a great deal of thought to how I present ideas during our television visits, and I'm always fascinated to hear how people have used what we have said. Often they use our ideas in creative, productive ways I had never dreamed they could be used.

So may it be with my words in the quotations that follow, which we've gathered from my speeches, newspaper columns, books, and television programs. May they find their place in the innermost part of you—in that essential part of you that inspires you to be who you really are.

• There's only one person in the whole world like you. If you think about it for a moment, there never has been—and there never will be—another person just like you.

• We're all so much alike, and yet we're all so different! I rejoice at the endless variety of people, and that's partly, I know, because these differences tell me that it's all right for me to be different in many ways, too.

• I think that everybody, every day, should be able to feel some success.

• You can't really love someone else unless you really love yourself first.

• Being perfectly human means having imperfections. All the same, most of us strive mightily to be lovable in the eyes of those we love. What those eyes tell us while we are infants are the most important messages we get about the value of being who we are.

• Nothing can replace the influence of unconditional love in the life of a child.

• In the disappointment of a defeat, a child may seem to find little comfort in our saying, "But you really tried hard, and I'm proud of you." It takes time to get over disappointment. For those children who have learned to feel valued and loved by the people they love, these disappointments do pass. It's the children who are less fortunate, those who feel they have to bank everything on their performance, who come to believe that losing in a competition means being one of life's unloved "losers."

• When we love a person, we accept him or her exactly as is: the lovely with the unlovely, the strong along with the fearful, the true mixed in with the facade. Of course, the only way we can do it is by accepting ourselves that way.

• We all need to feel that we have gifts that are valued.

• We serve children best when we try to find out what their own inner needs are and what their own unique endowments are, and to help them capitalize on that.

Fred Rogers, creator of "Mister Rogers' Neighborhood," is founder and president of Family Communications, Inc.

13

Reap a Destiny

by MaryLou Wendell Webb

F*rom the building* of a simple house, to the construction of an elaborate estate, the final product does not originate in the framing of the structure, or even in the drawing of plans, but in the heart and mind of the architect.

In the same way, when you have ideas and dreams for your own destiny, you have taken the first step toward achieving your goal. Nurture such thoughts, for they are proven building blocks of success. Our ideas, opinions, decisions, and notions about ourselves and the world around us shape our actions, and subsequently, our destinies. Consider this well-known maxim: Sow a thought, reap an action. Sow an action, reap a habit. Sow a habit, reap a character. Sow a character, reap a destiny.

Sow a Thought

When a farmer sows a crop, he first decides WHAT he wants to grow. In order to sow thoughts, you must first decide upon your desired outcome, and then sow your thoughts accordingly. For example, if your goal is to begin a new career, sow thoughts about the career that you have chosen. To do this, you could take stock of the qualities that you possess that will contribute to your success in your new career. Dwell on your strengths, while admitting your weaknesses. Pull out weeds of self-doubt and forgive past failures.

Realizing what you want out of life is the first step in directing your thoughts. Once you have set an ultimate goal, proactively choose your thoughts—do not let your thoughts choose you. This requires erasing all of the old, negative, self-demeaning tapes that play themselves in your head, and taking decisive control of every thought that enters your mind. These are tares that can strangle the life out of your precious crop. Learn to have a healthy view of yourself by recognizing your positive attributes. Those are the qualities that can take you anywhere you want to go. As you focus your mind, your thoughts will begin to take root, and you can begin to develop a course of action to achieve that ultimate goal.

Reap an Action

You can plan a vacation, research the sights, and make hotel reservations, but unless you actually get in the car and start driving, you won't go anywhere. Actions comprise most of an average person's day. To sow an action, you must first determine which of your daily actions are beneficial to you and the world around you, and which do not benefit anyone at all. Choose only the best actions possible, and do not settle for those that are merely good. Take actions that contribute to your ultimate destiny, remembering that character is the essence of success.

When it comes to our actions, most of us bite off more than we can chew. Schedules are overflowing, yet many actions could be weeded out by simply focusing on one's goals. Remember, every major goal is achieved through the achievement of several smaller goals. Think of it like a puzzle. Every time you find just two pieces that go together, you are closer to completing the bigger picture. When you realize that every little action that makes up even the smallest piece of the ultimate goal is important to complete, you find the process of achievement much more fulfilling on a daily basis. Daily actions are the building blocks of your destiny, and sowing the best of actions will result in strong and healthy habits.

Reap a Habit

It takes 21 days to form a habit. 21 DAYS! That means that whatever actions you are repeating day to day are habit forming—good or bad. If, for example, you tend to be five minutes late for work every day, and you persist in being five minutes late, you will form a bad habit. Every day that you continue the action, you reinforce the habit. If you are not intentionally forming good habits, you are probably unintentionally forming bad habits. The good news is, should you decide to take action, within 21 days—less than one month—you could not only break a bad habit, but replace it with a good one.

If the actions that you have sown are positive and successful actions, then the habits that you form will also be positive and successful. As you develop a structure of good habits, you will actually begin to realize the control you have over your destiny. More importantly, good habits will nourish your attitude, enhance your integrity, and bolster your self-worth.

Reap a Character

We started with a thought—WHY, moved into the action phase—WHAT, and have finally arrived at the most important aspect of choosing your destiny—WHO. It is your overall character that will truly determine your success. A highly motivated and determined person who has little or no strength of character may accomplish a great deal, but will never achieve success. WHO you are matters most of all, because circumstances are not always going to be in your favor, and there are many things that you cannot control; however, you can always control your character. It is with you wherever you go. It not only determines how you will treat others, but it determines how others will treat you in return.

A good character is easy to recognize, but not so easy to define. Many qualities come to mind—ethics, morals, good motives, strong convictions, a healthy attitude, a positive outlook, a humble heart, and an open mind—to name a few. These are the things that have no measure. There is no end, only a process. However, when you pursue the qualities of a strong character and combine them with your own natural personality, talents, and abilities, you will surely realize that your destiny is closer than ever!

MaryLou Wendell Webb is dean of the Management and Professional Development Division of Portland Community College.

14

Paths to Self-Mastery

by Kevin Cashman

W*hat does mastery* mean to you? Mastery is usually seen as mastery of something outside of ourselves. Our success tends to be measured by the degree to which we have mastered our external environment. But external results spring from the inner dynamics supporting peak performance.

When our lives are defined only in terms of the fruits of action, the circumstances of our lives define us. In this state of identity, we are fragile, vulnerable, and at-risk. Our core identity and passionate purpose are overshadowed by events. Success may even be present, but mastery has escaped us. We have chosen to "major" in the minor things in life.

Many of us are in a slumber. We go about our business and relationships much the same way day after day, rarely questioning where we are going and why. Often it takes a traumatic external event—a death, a termination, a divorce, a disease or a crisis—to bring us out of the depths of our slumber. But why wait to get shocked awake? Why not choose to wake up now?

Seven Pathways

Over the years we have identified seven pathways to awaken mastery. These constitute an integrated growth process, each supporting one another to guide our journey to a more masterful life.

• *Personal mastery.* If knowledge is power, then self-knowledge must be the source of real power. To do more, we first need to be more; to be more, we need to comprehend our being, our personhood. Understanding who we are and what we have to offer is the prerequisite for leveraging our capabilities. But most people are barreling down the freeway of life without comprehending the owner's manual of their "vehicle". Study your owner's manual: Objectively evaluate yourself. Begin the process of reconciling and integrating your strengths, weaknesses, and development needs.

• ***Purpose mastery.*** Purpose frames all of our life experiences into a meaningful whole. If we lack purpose, our circumstances dominate our awareness and overshadow our reason for being. As a result, our life tends to lose connection to its true nature. As Teilhard de Chardin wrote, "We are not human beings having a spiritual experience. We are spiritual beings having a human experience." Purpose is spirit seeking expression; it transforms everything it touches. To get in touch with purpose, identify three fulfilling experiences of your life. Then ask yourself: What meaningful contributions was I making during these experiences?

• ***Change mastery.*** Our personal evolution can be directly measured by our ability to adapt and to change. As Lao Tzu wrote, "Whatever is flexible and flowing will tend to grow; whatever is rigid and blocked will wither and die." We may need to focus more on opportunities; our short-term perspectives may need to shift to the longer term; our tendency to be absorbed in immediate circumstances may need to move to a more purpose-filled context; our need to be in control may need to become more flexible and adaptable; our doubt may need to be transformed to a more trusting, open attitude. Think about times when you faced major challenges. What qualities arose during those times? What were your key learnings?

• ***Career mastery.*** As Studs Terkel put it, "Most of us have jobs too small for our spirits." Is our current job big enough for our spirit? If it is, each task, responsibility and challenge can be a new opportunity to engage our purpose. If not, we may be earning a living but losing a life. Many people sacrifice their career fulfillment on the altar of security. To get on the path to career mastery, explore the most enjoyable, fulfilling "peaks" in your career. What were you doing? What skills were you using? Who were you working with? Why were these experiences so fulfilling to you?

• *Balance mastery.* Regardless of our level of external success, our life is precarious in the absence of balance. Without balance, every new opportunity or change could upset our gyroscope. High-performance people are especially vulnerable to imbalance. Each of us must find our own way to the dynamic balance supporting enhanced effectiveness and fulfillment. To sort out your own unique balancing act, ask yourself: "Are my personal and professional lives congruent with my principles and values?" There's no greater imbalance than to be disconnected from what is important to us.

• *Interpersonal mastery.* Nearly all effectiveness and fulfillment happen in relation to others. But how do we enhance our ability to relate? Our relationships always begin with our self-relationship. We can only give what we have. Once we have increased our inner value through self-mastery, we can build our emotional equity with others by focusing on the needs of others; become more adept at questioning and listening to sort out people's real needs and motivations. Then ask: What can I draw from within myself to meet these needs?

• *Being mastery.* Our fast-moving, never-catch-your-breath, externally focused culture is "perfectly" designed to avoid the silence of inner being. The background and foreground "noise" of our lives is so dominant, we rarely get a chance to connect with the silence deep within us. We have become human doers who have lost connection to our heritage as human beings. Connection with Inner Being provides us with the inner restfulness and peace to more effectively live in the eye of the hurricane of life. As Blaise Pascal wrote, "All man's miseries derive from not being able to sit quietly in a room alone." Consider learning how to meditate; connecting with the vastness of nature; relaxing to beautiful music.

By progressing along each pathway, we can advance from a focus on external achievement to multidimensional effectiveness and fulfillment.

Kevin Cashman is president of LeaderSource, a Minneapolis-based executive coaching consultancy, and author of *Leadership from the Inside Out.*

15

Principled Success

by Bob Briner

I*f you want* to succeed, study, learn, and apply the principles of Jesus Christ. The life and teachings of Jesus are packed full of wisdom highly relevant to my world and yours.

1. Have a plan. Few people have a master plan with short-term, intermediate, and long-range goals by which they chart their course and measure their progress. Jesus had a plan and adhered to it unfailingly. This is a major reason for his success. He knew where he was going, and he went there. Nothing deterred him. A plan puts you in charge of your energies and activities. You become proactive, not reactive. Without a plan, you have nowhere to go, nothing toward which to direct your energies.

2. Be prepared. Jesus prepared for 30 years before beginning to execute his plan. To ensure maximum effectiveness, the fullest realization of our plans, we must commit to the necessary preparation. Inadequate preparation produces inadequate results. Whether you're laying the foundation for a career, launching a product, or making a presentation, there is no substitute for preparation.

There is one thing you can count on in life—tough times will come. The wise person prepares for them. Many people who once had great success were wiped out when the tough times came because they were not prepared for them. Jesus continually prepared himself and his followers for the tough times. He warned them that the trials would come. His preparation paid off to an extraordinary degree.

3. Insist on absolutes. From pontificating pundits and tweedy talk show academics who have never met a payroll, we hear that it is not politically correct to insist on absolutes. Please don't try to run your life by this nonsense. Jesus insisted that some things are true and others false, that some things are right and others wrong, that some things are good and others evil. A lack of absolutes can lead to all kinds of problems, from petty thievery to major crimes.

4. Learn a little humility. In my own career, I have seen examples of unbelievable arrogance. I am sure I have displayed an unseemly amount myself. I have also seen this arrogance come back to haunt those who came to believe in their own invulnerability. I have seen dozens of people come into power, become mesmerized by their corporate sway, become unbearably arrogant, and then fall when the inevitable shifts knock them aside. Don't fall into the trap of arrogance. One way to combat it is to keep a picture in your mind of Jesus Christ, God's perfect son, kneeling before ordinary men, his own disciples, and washing their feet. With this picture in mind, it is hard to be arrogant.

5. Say "Thanks". Golfing great Jack Nicklaus is legendary for saying thanks. As he became a superstar, Nicklaus continued to look for ways to express his gratitude, and it has paid off in many ways for him.

You will note that Jesus always gave thanks for food before he ate. He was exceedingly thankful to his Father for the power his disciples demonstrated. It is impossible to say "thank you" too many times, so say it often.

6. Stay in touch with real people. Jesus touched lives in every level of society. He had many discourses with the leaders of his day, but he chose humble men as his closest associates. He traveled with, spoke to, and cared for people of every class. Don't lose touch with real people leading real lives.

7. Be responsive. Nowhere do we find Jesus telling someone to wait. He never said, "I'll get back to you." He never put anyone on hold. Jesus took care of matters on the spot. He answered questions, turned water into wine, fed the multitudes, and healed the sick of body and soul instantaneously. Of course, we don't have the perfect insight and miraculous power of Jesus, but we should follow his example. Unresponsiveness has all too often become the norm. It seems that fewer people return phone calls or answer their mail in a timely way.

8. Practice public speaking. Jesus, of course, was a masterful public speaker. He drew large crowds everywhere he spoke. Any list of great public discourses would have to include the Sermon on the Mount. It is a classic of both poetic beauty and powerful content.

Don't be a dull, boring, tiresome speaker. Find yourself a peer who will honestly critique your performances. Hire an outside consultant if necessary. Make sure he or she knows you want to get better, not flattered. Don't waste your opportunities to speak in public. Use the platform both to inspire and inform.

9. Be a servant. Jesus repeatedly emphasized servanthood, the idea that the way to succeed is to put others first. Many hard-charging types see this approach as sentimental, even otherworldly. The conventional wisdom is that to be number one, you must take care of number one. The reality is, however, that the surest way to success is to put other people first—in effect, to become a servant to them.

10. Get away from it all. Even with all Jesus had to accomplish during his short stay on earth, he still took plenty of time off. He made sure he had time alone for prayer and reflection. He got his sleep. There were times when everyone else was awake, but Jesus was sleeping. As always, he is a great example for us. It may seem politically savvy and the macho thing to be thought of as a go-go guy, never resting, never getting away. But a well-rested person always accomplishes more than a tired, stressed-out person. Take your vacations, real vacations—ones in which you truly do get away from the office. Jesus valued time away, time alone. You should too.

To succeed, use the Jesus model. Take good care of yourself and your customers. When Jesus said, "He who is greatest among you shall be your servant," he made a statement by which any person can live and thrive.

Bob Briner is a television producer and the author of *The Management Methods of Jesus.*

16

Do You Have What It Takes to Succeed?

by Albert Bandura

People *with high* assurance in their capabilities (strong self-efficacy) approach difficult tasks as challenges to be mastered rather than as threats to be avoided.

They set themselves challenging goals and maintain strong commitment to them. They heighten and sustain their efforts in the face of failure. They quickly recover their sense of efficacy after failures or setbacks. They attribute failure to insufficient effort or deficient knowledge and skills, which are acquirable. They approach threatening situations with assurance that they can exercise control over them. Such a positive outlook produces personal achievements, reduces stress, and lowers vulnerability to depression.

In contrast, people who doubt their capabilities shy away from difficult tasks, which they view as personal threats. They have low aspirations and weak commitment to the goals they choose to pursue. When faced with difficult tasks, they dwell on their deficiencies, on the obstacles they will encounter and on adverse outcomes rather than concentrate on how to perform successfully. They slacken their efforts and give up quickly in the face of difficulties. They are slow to recover their sense of efficacy following failure or setbacks. Because they view insufficient performance as deficient aptitude, failure causes them to lose faith in their capabilities. They fall easy victims to stress and depression.

Four Sources of Self-Efficacy

People's beliefs about their efficacy are developed through four main sources of influence.

1. Mastery experiences. The most effective way of creating a strong sense of efficacy is through mastery experiences. Successes build a robust belief in our personal efficacy. Failures undermine it, especially if failures occur before our sense of efficacy is firmly established.

If we experience only easy successes, we come to expect quick results and are easily discouraged by failure. A resilient sense of efficacy requires experience in overcoming obstacles through perseverance. Some setbacks and difficulties in our pursuits serve a useful purpose in teaching that success usually requires sustained effort. After we become convinced we have what it takes to succeed, we persevere in the face of adversity and quickly rebound from setbacks.

2. Vicarious experiences. The second way of creating and strengthening self-beliefs of efficacy is through the vicarious experiences provided by social models. Seeing people similar to us succeed by sustained effort raises our beliefs that we too possess the capabilities to master comparable activities. By the same token, observing others fail despite high effort lowers our judgments of our own efficacy and undermines our efforts. The impact of modeling on perceived self-efficacy is strongly influenced by perceived similarity to the models. The greater the assumed similarity, the more persuasive are the models' successes and failures. If we see the models as very different from ourselves, our perceived self-efficacy is not much influenced by the models' behavior and the results they produce.

Modeling influences do more than provide a social standard against which to judge our own capabilities. We seek proficient models who possess the competencies to which we aspire. Through their behavior and expressed ways of thinking, competent models transmit knowledge and teach us effective skills strategies for managing environmental demands.

3. Social persuasion. A third way of strengthening our beliefs that we have what it takes to succeed is through social persuasion. People who are persuaded verbally that they possess the capabilities to master given activities are likely to mobilize greater effort and sustain it than if they harbor self-doubts and dwell on personal deficiencies when problems arise. To the extent that persuasive boosts in perceived self-efficacy lead people to try hard enough to succeed, they promote development of skills and a sense of personal efficacy.

It is more difficult to instill high beliefs of personal efficacy by social persuasion alone than to undermine it. Unrealistic boosts in efficacy are quickly disconfirmed by disappointing results of one's efforts. But people who have been persuaded that they lack capabilities tend to avoid challenging activities that cultivate potentialities and give up quickly in the face of difficulties. By constricting activities and undermining motivation, disbelief in one's capabilities creates its own behavioral validation.

Successful efficacy builders do more than convey positive appraisals. In addition to raising people's beliefs in their capabilities, they structure situations for them in ways that bring success and avoid placing people in situations prematurely where they are likely to fail often. They measure success in terms of self-improvement rather than by triumphs over others.

4. Somatic and emotional states. People also rely partly on their somatic and emotional states in judging their capabilities. They interpret their stress reactions and tension as signs of vulnerability to poor performance. In activities involving strength and stamina, people judge their fatigue, aches, and pains as signs of physical debility. Mood also has an effect. Positive mood enhances perceived self-efficacy, and despondent mood diminishes it.

Reducing our stress reactions and altering our negative emotional proclivities modifies self-beliefs of efficacy. It is not the sheer intensity of emotional and physical reactions that is important but rather how they are perceived and interpreted. People who have a high efficacy are more likely to view their state of affective arousal as an energizing facilitator of performance.

Albert Bandura is a renowned psychologist and teacher at Stanford University. He is also the author of many books, including *Self-Efficacy: An Exercise in Control.*

17

Winding Up

by Jimmy and Rosalynn Carter

A*s we approach* retirement age, we naturally have more frequent and somber thoughts about the end of our lives, although all the great religions teach us not to fear death. But perhaps it is even more important not to be afraid of advancing age. This late period can be a time of foreboding and resignation, a time merely of assessment and contemplation. But it also offers the chance to be bolder than ever before and to do worthwhile things that have been avoided or postponed.

Retirement can be one of life's greatest dangers if all we do is brace ourselves to face what we think will be many barren and useless years.

As we have tried to show, longer life and earlier retirement can create significant new opportunities. A second career can be gratifying because it is built upon many years of experience, accumulated knowledge, influence, and perhaps freedom from financial uncertainty. This career warrants as much careful thought and planning as we gave our first one. This period may also offer the first chance to repay our community by service and sharing, for which there had previously never been the time.

At any time in life, it is appropriate to ponder the question "For me, what is success?" We should inventory our talents and interests, that our goals in life should be worthy as measured by God, that we should attempt things that might be beyond our abilities, and that this would put us in a spirit of submission to God's will. Once we do all this, we can then undertake worthy goals with boldness and confidence, realizing that these revised ambitions might be quite different from the more self-serving achievements we had previously coveted.

One lesson we have learned over the years is how much our everyday decisions affect our long-term health and happiness. There is a great temptation while we are in the thick of things to postpone doing what we would either like to do or ought to do.

We can also add vitality to our lives by actively experimenting with new interests, tasks, and hobbies. Over the years we have tried photography, woodworking, gardening, gourmet cooking, fly-fishing, oil painting, bird watching, collecting old bottles and Indian artifacts, building houses, writing books, and a wide range of sports—cross-country and Alpine skiing, tennis, jogging, bowling, mountain trekking, windsurfing, and biking.

We make new friends by sharing our interests with others, especially those who have mastered the techniques.

We find it satisfying not only to do a lot of our own yard work and the repairs and renovations in our home but also to design and build cabinets and furniture, lay a new hardwood floor, do rudimentary plumbing and masonry jobs, and rewire the hi-fi sound system. Also, we are frequently in our woods and fields.

For us, promoting good for others has made a tremendous difference in our lives in recent years. There are serious needs everywhere for volunteers who want to help those who are hungry, homeless, blind, crippled, addicted to drugs or alcohol, illiterate, mentally ill, elderly, imprisoned, or just friendless and lonely. For most of us, learning about these people, who are often our immediate neighbors, can add a profound new dimension to what might otherwise be a time of worrying too much about ourselves.

There is no way to know how many years we will have to spend together, and we want to make the most of them.

Jimmy and Rosalynn Carter are the former President and First Lady of the United States of America, respectively.

18

Moving On

by Pat Riley

The renewals I have experienced have usually moved me around to different places and organizations, but that need not always be the case. It is certainly harder to "move on" while you stay in the same place, because all of the cues and relationships are there to reinforce the old behaviors, but it certainly can be done. But sometimes "moving on" means literally moving on.

When I moved from Los Angeles to New York, even before I arrived, people asked me, "What is it going to be like in New York?" And I always answered, "I know one thing. It's going to be exhilarating."

The changes in my life have not always gone in the directions I hoped for, but they have always taken me to places and situations where I could learn and grow.

In 1963 I drove from New York to Kentucky, where I was blessed with one of the greatest coaches in basketball history, Adolph Rupp. Then the NBA draft brought me to the San Diego Rockets. There I met the woman who would become my wife.

Then I was sent to Portland, and seemed on my way out of the league when a near-fluke decision by the Lakers put me on a team that was to become the winningest group in the history of pro sports.

Then, after being cut and having to learn how to dismiss my bitterness and envy, I found myself doing the production and broadcasting work that drew me back to the Lakers.

With each move and change, there was fear. With each, I scarcely appreciated its importance when it happened. But somehow every step led me to a better place.

There is only one real alternative for the winners within, and that is moving on. It is to search out new teams, goals, and challenges—either in the same place or in a new setting.

Properly understood, moving on is not a retreat from defeat, but an exhilarating change that makes you feel vital and alive.

Pat Riley, a former NBA player, coach, and broadcaster, is the author of *The Winner Within.*

19

Obedience to the Unenforceable

by John Silber

Some 75 years ago, John Fletcher Moulton, a noted English judge, spoke on the subject of "Law and Manners." He divided human action into three domains.

The first is ***the domain of law,*** "where," he said, "our actions are prescribed by laws binding upon us which must be obeyed." At the other extreme is the ***domain of free choice,*** "which," he said, "includes all those actions as to which we claim and enjoy complete freedom." And in between Lord Moulton identified a domain in which our action is not determined by law but in which we are not free to behave in any way we choose. In this domain we act with greater or lesser freedom from constraint.

Lord Moulton considered the area of action between law and pure personal preference to be ***"the domain of obedience to the unenforceable."*** This domain between law and free choice he called that of Manners. While it may include moral duty, social responsibility and proper behavior, it extends beyond them to cover "all cases of doing right where there is no one to make you do it but yourself."

Obedience to law does not alone measure a nation's greatness. The true test of greatness, Moulton said, is "the extent to which individuals can be trusted to obey self-imposed law."

Today the domains of choice and of law have eroded the domain of manners. As the realm of manners and morals has been diminished by those who claim that whatever they think or do is right if it feels good to them, the central domain loses its force.

It is against the law to deface public property, to steal, to swindle, to drive while intoxicated, to rape, to bomb and to kill. But our public and private buildings are regularly defaced by graffiti and the territorial markings of juvenile gangs. In our cities, many feel imprisoned in their homes, and our persons are at risk on our streets and in our parks. Rape is epidemic and deadly assault by drunken drivers is commonplace. Nor is the crime wave confined to the streets: The *Wall Street Journal* estimates that stock swindles and other forms of white-collar crime cost Americans $100 billion every year.

But what of enforcement? Indictments number only a small fraction of the crimes committed, convictions only a fraction of the indictments. Standards in law have eroded, as lawyers and juries have become less obedient to the unenforceable. Judges frequently exclude from jury duty persons of education and competence.

Even more alarming than the comedy of the courts is the tragedy of the streets: the random violence, the children killed in drive-by shootings by persons they have never met, and acts of terrorism which demonstrate the inability of a sovereign nation to protect the lives and property of its citizens.

We cannot end this state of violence and restore the authority of law simply by getting tough on crime, by relying on the police power of the state, or by calling for capital punishment.

Authority and civil order depend in a significant measure on the consent of the governed—that is, on obedience to the unenforceable. The more civilized and enlightened the country, the greater its dependence on the voluntary respect and support of its citizens for law and civil order. The rule of law depends upon the morality of the people.

Obedience to the unenforceable is required to give to the rule of law the power of enforcement. The law is not self-sustaining, but depends like science, medicine, higher education, and accounting, on the willingness of scientists, doctors, professors, lawyers and accountants to obey moral principles that are unenforceable. The integrity and efficacy of all our professions and businesses rest on this moral foundation.

We must not attribute all our social ills to a single cause, however, for the causes are many. If families had not broken up, if churches had not lost much of their influence, if there had not been an extensive spread of secularism and materialism, if the quality of our schools had not declined, if drugs had not been easily available, we might have withstood the degenerative effects of television and its indiscriminate advocacy of pleasure.

Common sense alone tells us that violence endlessly enacted on television serves as a model for imitation. Recognizing that by its nature, obedience to the unenforceable cannot be enforced, W. Edwards Deming observed, "You don't have to do it—survival is not compulsory."

A Crisis of Spirit

We face a crisis of the spirit. Its resolution far transcends the power of the state; it is too important, too far-reaching, to be resolved by mere governmental action. Rather, it lies within the grasp of each of us. When we determine to govern ourselves—when each is obedient to the unenforceable—we shall regain control over ourselves and thus regain as a nation our capacity for self-government.

This will never come to pass, however, without faith in the importance of honor and truth and in the essential role of duty and obligation in our lives. What we are, what we do and thereby what we become depends heavily on what we believe about ourselves. Are we Edwin Markham's man with a hoe, "A thing that grieves not and that never hopes, stolid and stunned, a brother to the ox"?

Or are we not rather "the Thing the Lord God made and gave To have dominion over sea and land; To trace the stars and search the heavens for power, To feel the passion of Eternity?"

The future of our country, our future happiness, depends decisively on whether we as individuals practice obedience to the unenforceable.

John Silber is president of Boston University.

20

Four Keys to Success

by Harvey Mackay

How *do you* become a truly successful person? For me, success has four parts:

1. Never stop learning. Some time ago, I attended a tennis camp in Arizona. I've played tennis most of my life, but I'm still not as good as I want to be. So I go to camps.

One morning I was assigned to play a doubles match. Four people showed up and partners were decided by spinning a racket. As luck would have it, I wound up with a 92-year-old. I wondered how things would work out, but I shouldn't have worried. The first two sets, we hammered our opponents 6-1, 6-1!

My partner was totally amazing. As we were switching sides to play the third set, he said to me: "Do you mind if I play the backhand court? I always like to work on my weaknesses." What a fantastic example of a person who has never stopped learning. Incidentally, we also hammered them in the third set 6-1.

As we walked off the court that day, my 92-year-old partner chuckled and said to me: "I thought you might like to know that I am ranked number one in the United States, in my age bracket, the 85 years old and up!" You see, he wasn't thinking 92, he wasn't even thinking 85. He was thinking number one.

You can do the same if you have the discipline to work on your weaknesses and develop your strengths, if you have the will to learn and the self-confidence that comes of knowing you're prepared to handle the pressure. You'll always have the edge if you think number one.

A goal is a dream with a deadline: measurable, identifiable, attainable, and in writing. Remember, pale ink is better than the most retentive memory. Write your goals down.

2. ***Believe in yourself, even when no one else does.*** Don't ever let anyone tell you you can't accomplish your goals. Who says you're not tougher, better, harder working, and more able than your competition? It doesn't matter if they say you can't do it. The only thing that matters is if you say it. If you believe in yourself, there's hardly anything you can't do. If you prepare to win, and believe that you can win, you will be a winner.

A few months ago I was in New York and hailed a taxi. It turned out to be a most memorable ride. Most New York cab drivers are unfriendly, if not downright rude. Most cabs are filthy, and almost all of them sport an impenetrable bullet-proof partition. This time, I jumped into a cab at LaGuardia Airport, and it was a clean cab. There was beautiful music coming out of the sound system and, believe it or not, no bulletproof partition.

I said to the driver, "Park Lane Hotel, please." He turned around with a big, broad smile and said, "Hi, my name is Wally," and he handed me a mission statement. That's right, a mission statement! It said he was going to get me there safely, courteously, and on time.

As he pulled away from the curb he held up copies of the *New York Times* and *USA Today* and said, "Be my guest." A few minutes into the ride he motioned to me not to be bashful and to help myself to some of the fruit in the basket on the back seat. He then promptly asked if I preferred to listen to rock and roll or classical music from his audiotape collection. About 10 minutes into the ride he held up a cellular telephone and said, "It's a dollar a minute if you would like to make a call."

Somewhat shocked, I blurted out, "Where did you learn this?" He answered, "On a talk show." I then asked, "How long have you been practicing this?" And he answered, "Three or four years." I then said, "I know this is prying, but would you mind sharing with me how much extra money you earn in tips?" He responded proudly: "From $12,000 to $14,000 a year!"

This man is my hero. He's living proof that you can always shift the odds in your favor if you believe in yourself.

3. Find a way to make a difference. Robert Redford has been a great example of this. If anybody has the perfect job, he does. But, unlike so many successful people, Redford remembers where he came from. Instead of asking, "What's in it for me?" he asks, "What can I give back?" His desire to give back to his industry led to the creation of the Sundance Institute. Sundance is a haven in the mountains of Utah where Redford has given his time, his talent, his money, and his land to create opportunities for young people to become filmmakers. "Fellows" come from all over the world to collaborate with the best writers, directors, and producers the American film industry has to offer.

The most lasting legacy any human being can leave is to give someone else a boost on the way up. This is truly Robert Redford at his best. You, too, can find a way to make a difference.

4. Eat the heart of the watermelon. When I was a kid, my father knew a guy named Bernie who had started out his career with a vegetable stand, worked hard all his life, and eventually became wealthy as a wholesaler. Every summer, when the first good watermelons came in, Dad would take me down to Bernie's warehouse and we'd have a feast. Bernie would choose a couple of watermelons, crack them open, and hand each of us a big piece. Then, with Bernie taking the lead, we'd eat only the heart of the watermelon—the reddest, juiciest, most perfect part—and throw the rest away.

My father never made a lot of money. We were raised to clean our plates and not waste food. Bernie was my father's idea of a rich man. And I always thought it was because he'd been such a success in business. My father admired Bernie's "richness" because he knew how to stop work in the middle of a summer, day, sit down with his friends, and eat the heart of the watermelon.

Being rich is a state of mind. Some of us, no matter how much money we have, will never be free enough to take the time to stop and eat the heart of the watermelon. And some of us will be rich without ever being more than a paycheck ahead of the game.

Harvey Mackay is CEO of Mackay Envelope and author of *Dig Your Well Before You Are Thirsty.*

SECTION 3

Meeting Challenges

21

The Champion Within

by Bruce Jenner

The annals of glory are filled with tales of bottle rockets, men and women who fire fast and soar high, then come crashing to the ground in an even more startling explosion of fire and noise and light.

I never thought that could happen to me. But it did.

Most people remember me as the Bicentennial Olympic champion who seemed too All-American to be true, the Bruce Jenner of the Wheaties box and the *Sports Illustrated* cover. Well, you wouldn't have recognized me in 1990.

I was living in the hills outside of Los Angeles, in a one-bedroom bungalow where the dirty dishes filled the kitchen sink and a dried-out Christmas tree from the holidays four months ago sat in a clump beside the door, serving as the only attempt at interior decoration. I'd lost between 15 and 20 pounds, and years of physical inactivity had left me looking thin. I probably needed a haircut but, living alone with nobody to talk to, I would have been the last to know. I had just celebrated my 40th birthday, and I desperately needed help. I'd lost all direction in life. I'd lost interest in business. And after two bad marriages, I didn't even want to think about dating. My self-esteem wasn't exactly soaring. In fact, I thought I was so unattractive that I spent thousands of dollars I didn't have on a nose job, only to have the surgeon botch it so badly he had to do it all over again. So much for self-improvement.

Between personal appearances, my life consisted mostly of golf and learning to play a rented piano, leaving me lots of idle time. I had $200 in the bank and debts of about $500,000. My main source of income was talking about the Games, about how I once was a winner, the man proclaimed the World's Greatest Athlete, while valiantly not letting on how much and how long I'd been losing. For somebody who'd won so much professionally, it was amazing how much I was suffering personally. I hoped that nobody could see the defeat and loneliness.

In so many ways, I was still the dyslexic kid who lived in fear of being called upon to get up in front of the class and read. I was right back where I started: stripped of self-esteem, doubting my abilities to make intelligent decisions, and failing in every area of my life.

Light and Love

I had grown accustomed to a life without: without intimacy, without excitement, without adventure, without growth. I was broken as a man. And my medal, the golden symbol of all that I had won, sat in a drawer, now the symbol of how much I'd lost.

Wherever you are in your own life, no matter how low you've sunk, I can empathize. I've been there. I had given up. I had lost my will. But once I hit bottom, I remembered something from my past: there's no place for losers in sport or in life.

The champion who lives inside each of us, the champion who had the capacity to stand before the world in victory, would no longer allow me to live this lifestyle. I had to get out! And once I did, once I decided to play the game of life, something extraordinary happened.

I saw light at the end of the tunnel. It arrived in the form of the love of my life and soulmate, my wife Kris. Suddenly, I realized that I could turn my life around and start anew with a clean slate. Kris reintroduced me to the power that I had experienced, but never understood, so many years before at the Olympic Games. It was a power that I could fully comprehend only after I had sunk into the pit of misery. It was a power that would drive me back to the top with a speed that exceeded anything I'd experienced before.

It was the power of the champion within. Once again, I could see my goal in front of me, close enough to reach out and grab. Once again, the clock in my head ticked incessantly. This time, the goal had rewards unconnected with sport; this time the goal was personal. Absolute personal glory, the gold medal in human development, to become the best person—husband, father, businessman, contributor—I could possibly become. Once again when I could see my goal I could focus exclusively on it.

Now, years after leaving my solitary existence, my life has blossomed with an amazing ferocity; it was like the angels arrived, the skies parted, and the seas split, allowing me to run through. I have taken my gold medal out of my sock drawer and proudly mounted it upon the wall, allowing it to shine brightly in every area of my life.

For the first time in my life, I know what love means. I thought that it was something unattainable, something that I didn't deserve. Now I know that it is the seed from which all great things grow.

I have discovered that our performance in life is a direct reflection of the image we have of ourselves. Now I look as good as I feel. I get up every morning eager to tackle my day. From loving my wife to having a meaningful relationship with my kids to being totally fulfilled in business, life has never been better. I am in the best physical shape since I competed in the games over 20 years ago. But now I'm not merely in touch with my body but also my heart. And when those two feelings meet, a combustible reaction occurs, allowing me, at 48, to enter a realm I never thought possible.

Now I am on a new mission, a mission to share my experiences and help people realize the potential that lies deep inside. In this way, my victory may become more than one note in the history books. It may become a victory that gives something back, allowing me to help others realize that no matter what their situation in life, they have the power to move forward and make life a great adventure. As Helen Keller once said, "Life is either a daring adventure or nothing."

Somewhere out there, your stadium is waiting, filled with all the people you love. They are rooting for you as you struggle, and they'll be cheering as you finally come around the backstretch and finish as a champion.

Getting Started

Deep within each of us lies a power, a power forever beginning to be awakened. Getting started is merely a matter of following a few very basic, simple rules:

1. Recognize the champion within. Realize that deep inside of you a champion is waiting, ready to rise and radically transform every aspect of your existence.

2. Find your arena to play in. Look at finding your life's purpose as an excavation; you might not find the answer the first time you dig. But keep digging. Begin with your dreams. Visualize yourself as a champion—the ultimate peak performer—and ask yourself, "Where would that champion play if he or she could play anywhere in the world?" Look at your surroundings and see if there is room for that champion to play where you are. If not, where do you have to go for the champion to reach full potential?

3. Once you've found your arena, enter it. Don't hesitate. Take that first step. Go with what you've got at your disposal and give it your all. If it doesn't work out, don't quit. Merely reframe your mission and move on.

4. Rewire your brain regarding the word "failure." You can find something in your present that can jump-start your future. Know that failure is but a temporary stumble in the race and that every successful mission is the final result of endless missteps. As my friend Barry Farber writes, "There is never a straight line between where we are now and where we want to be. But a mistake, a failure or a negative thought is just another bend in the road. Go beyond that bend and you're that much closer to your destination. Give up when you hit a rocky patch, and you'll never reach your goal."

5. Cut off all lines of escape. Put yourself in a situation where the only answer is action! Vow total commitment to your cause.

Bruce Jenner is an Olympic gold medalist, motivational speaker, and TV personality. He is the author of *Finding the Champion Within.*

22

We Can Move Mountains

by Montel Williams

M*y beliefs are* fairly straightforward, and not uncommon. If you reject my beliefs, that's fine, but here they are: I believe in God. I believe in love and family. I believe in education. I believe in hard work and dedication. I believe in restraint, respect, and responsibility. I believe in love and romance. And I believe in setting goals and reaching them. There is nothing you can't do if you set your mind to it.

My conviction and the constant theme of my life is this: "Mountain, get out of my way." It's a line I first heard in Marine Corps boot camp. I had a drill instructor who used to say it all the time. By the time I left boot camp it was a part of me. There is no more important message. If you have faith, you can move mountains. If you have faith in something bigger than yourself—in God, community, family—then anything is possible. Faith will give you the strength to clear any obstacle in your way.

I'm the youngest of four children, born when and where it wasn't easy for a black man to earn an honest living. I'm the product of a loving home, splintered by tension and frustration. My father worked three or four jobs. My mother worked two. They barely had time for themselves, let alone for us kids. My sisters and brother and I all worked when we were old enough. We went to church every Sunday. We ate dinner together most evenings. There were no shortcuts.

From One Generation to the Next

In a message to my son, I mentioned things I can pass on to him. They are:

I will give you the tools that I wish I had growing up. I will teach you the three Rs: restraint, respect, and responsibility. I will teach you discipline, love, tolerance, faith, and forgiveness. Some of these things I do not yet know for myself, but I will learn them, for you. I will be here for you, in every way I can. This is my promise.

I don't want us to be like the father and son in Harry Chapin's song "Cat's in the Cradle." It's about a father who works his tail off, trying to provide for his family, and he wakes up one day to find his kids are grown and into busy lives of their own. But I can understand the father's dilemma. Sometimes I stumble home late, thrashed from an out-of-town trip, and pull you into bed with me, to sleep on my stomach. Or, I'll wake you up early, to throw the ball around, if that's the only time we'll have to be together that day.

I work so hard right now—and sometimes I lose sight of what I'm working for: the freedom to be around for you in ways my father could not be around for me. Since the moment you opened your eyes in the delivery room, I have felt a profound sense of responsibility and purpose.

I love you, Montel. I truly do. It may be that we get so caught up in the discipline and routine that we both lose sight of this beautiful truth, but I hope not, and if we do, at least you'll have it here, for the record. Your father loves you more than life itself. I would give up my life for you. I would stop a bullet for you. I'd do the same for your sisters and your mother.

That you carry my name is a blessing, but it might also be a curse. Your mother and I thought a long time about this, but in the end we decided that I am who I am, and you will be who you will be. My failures will not be yours, just as my successes will not be yours. I can't turn over any family business to you or groom you to replace me. Even if I could, I wouldn't, because I don't think a man can respect himself until he makes his own way. You've got to build your own future. You've got to keep your eyes open and focused—not on what I've done, but on what you can do.

I hope to guide you, teach you, mentor you, shape you, but I'm no role model. Your role model should be your own two eyes, staring back in the mirror. That is the shining example of who you should be and what you can become. Be ever vigilant in everything you do. Look ahead. Look around. Know where you're going all the time. Know how it makes you feel. Know that you deserve respect. Demand it, and if you don't get it, move on.

Above all, know that you have the hope of God in you, that you are placed on this planet to be the best that you can be. Look at yourself in the mirror and like what you see. Be proud. Know who you are. And know that I'll be looking back at you, always. Remember: I am your legacy; you are my future. Together we can move mountains.

Montel Williams hosts his own talk show and is the author of *Mountain, Get Out of My Way.*

23

Slaying the Dragon

by Michael Johnson

I *am not* by nature a daydreamer. I try to control those parts of my life that can be controlled, to plan everything that I want to happen down to the most insignificant detail. I traffic in a world in which fractions of a second separate success and failure, so I crafted a decade of dreams into ambitions, refined ambitions into goals, and finally hammered goals into plans. There were countless repetitions in the weight room and intervals on the track, exhilarating victories and debilitating losses, events that followed plans and others that ruined them.

Ten years of my life led to this achievement: gold medal in the 400 meters and gold medal in the 200 meters, the first man ever to win Olympic gold in those two very different races.

Ten years ago, I had run the same distance in 21 seconds, good for a high school athlete but well short of world class. A decade of tireless work and complete dedication had earned me little more than 1.5 seconds. A second and a half! That was the difference between being mediocre and being the fastest in the world. Barely time for a breath, and inhale and exhale. No more than a whisper for perfection.

Quest for Perfection

Perfection. In the end, I suppose that's why I run, not just for the other runners on the track or for the people in the stands or watching on television, not just because of the pressure inside or out, certainly not just because of the records or the desire to make history. Those things are all part of it, of course, but the reason is larger than any of them. I just wonder sometimes: Is it possible to run a perfect race?

There is a saying among some athletes that after you have stared long enough into the dragon's eyes, there is nothing left to do but slay the dragon. For each of us, that dragon is the thing closest to the center of our lives. It is our core, our ambition, and our joy. For me, it is the perfect race.

Success is found in much smaller portions than most people realize, achieved through the tiniest gradations, not unlike the split-second progress of a sprinter. A hundredth of a second here or sometimes a tenth there can determine the fastest man in the world. Two calls might separate the best salesperson from the worst. One misspelling might determine the valedictorian. At times, we live our lives on a paper-thin edge that barely separates greatness from mediocrity and success from failure.

That sliver of performance is where you will find the rewards that come from a sprinter's training, from the confidence, discipline, and focus that I have honed my entire career. Life is often compared to a marathon, but I think it is more like being a sprinter: long stretches of hard work punctuated by brief moments in which we are given the opportunity to perform at our best.

I disagree with our culture's habit of creating instant role models out of athletes. And yet I am honored to be in that position. I have learned a great deal from others: from my family, from my coaches, and from a few heroes of my own, people like Jesse Owens and Muhammad Ali, who have inspired me through their example, through incredible victories and terrifying losses, throughout lives that were even more brilliant in their fullness than they were in their individual achievements.

To me, that's the ultimate responsibility and challenge of being a role model—not to sign autographs in a timely fashion or to live a stainless life, but to offer up a life or a philosophy, flaws and all, to help other people negotiate their own way. The Atlanta Olympics would never have happened for me without that first goal. It is the same with you. You'll never know how far you can go until you shave off that first hundredth of a second, until you run ceaselessly toward the edge.

I encourage you to identify what you really want and how to get there; to set goals based upon realism and confidence; to work with discipline and resolve; to learn from the requisite failures and the too-early successes; to achieve a clarity of focus and a sense of purpose; to stick to your plan; to deal with pressure, thrive on it, and make it your own; and, perhaps most important, to keep going after you lose the biggest race of your life. Because you will. But after each of those terrible losses you can retool your machine, regain your focus, and find another biggest race. And another. And another. I have only now realized: Even in the best race there will always be a slight stumble, a shudder, a hitch, always room for a hundredth of a second improvement. That is the great thing about being human. You can always go just a little bit faster.

I wish I could teach you how to achieve perfection, how to slay the dragon every time. Instead, I hope to show you something far more valuable: how to chase it.

I believe our best inspiration comes, not from the sophisticated adult desires for power or prestige or money, but from the simple adolescent dreams: Run fast, jump high, be in love, have fun.

I'm lucky that I was young when I realized what I am chasing—speed—the thing so close to my core that I'm willing to do all it takes to excel. If you are like most people, you might not find that essential desire, that core, until you're much older. You might never recognize it in yourself. We all know perfectly happy people in their fifties who say, "I don't know what I want to be when I grow up." I think that's incredibly healthy. There's no reason your chase can't change, your dreams adapt. When my running career is over, I plan to approach business with the same focus and energy, and when I marry and have children I plan to invest the same joy and hard work in my family life.

I believe the path that leads through self-discipline and order is the way to all sorts of diverse success and happiness, not just the way to winning.

Michael Johnson is a world champion sprinter, Olympic gold medalist, and author of *Slaying the Dragon.*

24

Overcoming Obstacles

by Mark Victor Hansen and Jack Canfield

S*o many people* struggle with negative attitudes and self-defeating behaviors because they fail to realize that what you think about comes about. If you don't discipline yourself to be positive by tuning in to positive messages and hanging out with positive people, then the world tends to suck the life-force out of you. Your output will always reflect your input. So if you have negative input, you are going to have negative results in your life. If you have positive input, you will have positive results.

When you felt down or sick as a child, your mother probably fed you chicken soup. One reason we wrote *Chicken Soup for the Soul* was to give people hope by telling stories about individuals who've overcome great obstacles.

Some obstacles are bigger than others and take longer to overcome. You can't do it all over a weekend. But you are only one good idea away from success, one good idea away from being rich, one good idea away from being healthy—and you make the decision.

In *A Third Serving of Chicken Soup for the Soul,* we have a masterful statement by Nelson Mandela. We wept when we heard it. He says, "Our deepest fear is not that we are inadequate. Our deepest fear is that we are powerful beyond measure. It is our light, not our darkness, that most frightens us. We ask ourselves, 'Who am I to be brilliant, gorgeous, talented or famous?' Actually, who are you not to be. You are a child of God. Your playing small does not serve the world."

It often takes a "prison experience" to produce greatness. You have to be down to be up later. We have faced our own tough times in the past, including a bankruptcy, so we understand down. And we also know something about how to bounce back. The transition starts by getting into solitude, into silence. It is only in silence of the soul that you get to meet God face-to-face, so to speak. It is in that silence that you see who you are and what your purpose is in life.

You may succeed by yourself, on your own, but in the end it gets hollow. The fact is we are spiritual beings, and we live in a spiritual world where there is much that we can't understand. Just being alive is a miracle.

Role for a Master Mind

Still, to achieve great things, we all need a coach or mentor. We coach each other. One of us is the macro thinker, and one the micro thinker. You need both in a good partnership. You also need to commit to somebody that you are going to make it happen. It is not possible otherwise. A flashlight doesn't work with one battery, and none of us works very well alone.

We feel that it's better to eat "chicken soup" as a cure for what ails you than to be fueled by taunts of "being chicken." But different things work for different people. Some people climb Mount Everest because someone told them they couldn't. But the people who are motivated by dares are a very small minority among the great achievers. What we need are models, not critics.

After reading *Chicken Soup for the Soul,* you feel better about yourself because you see that others have faced major obstacles and prevailed. We get over 100 letters a day from people who say, "I didn't think I was good enough" or "I was going to commit suicide" or "I didn't think I had it in me, but your story turned me around."

Obstacles only make life more exciting. All of us like the right kind of opposition and competition—we thrive on it. So why fear it when it serves to make us stronger and better?

Jack and I believe that human potential is vastly underestimated, and we believe that no one can succeed without overcoming real obstacles that stretch the soul. "Effort only fully releases its reward after a person refuses to quit," said Napoleon Hill.

Recently, we traveled to Saskatchewan, Canada, to meet with an Indian tribe that has a high suicide rate. The chief urged us to share our stories with his people. It's universal. Everyone needs stories about overcoming obstacles to get them over the hard times.

Four Success Principles, Many Examples

When we speak to groups of people, we often share four basic principles of success: 1) you have to figure out what you want—not really, but ideally—in all areas of your life, including your health, happiness, relationships, and finances; 2) you've got to put it in writing—"I am going to be healthy by eating right and exercising 20 minutes a day"; 3) you've got to visualize it to realize it, and see it before you can have it; and 4) you've got to have your team together to get your dream together, meaning you have to have your mastermind (coach or mentor) and come together in harmony to create dynamic synergy.

Empowered people, working in cooperation, are what cause change in the world. America is a great country because those who succeed give other people a hand. Every millionaire in this country makes 11 more millionaires; and so the most unselfish thing you can do is become very successful.

B.C. Forbes noted, "History has demonstrated that the most notable winners usually encountered heartbreaking obstacles before they triumphed. They won because they refused to become discouraged by their defeats."

In our books are many stories of people who have overcome serious handicaps.

- After Fred Astaire's first screen test, the memo from the testing director of MGM, dated 1933, said, "Can't act! Slightly bald! Can dance a little!" Astaire kept that memo over the fireplace in his Beverly Hills home.
- An expert said of coach Vince Lombardi: "He possesses minimal football knowledge. Lacks motivation."
- The philosopher Socrates was called "an immoral corrupter of youth."
- Louisa May Alcott, the author of *Little Women,* was encouraged to find work as a servant or seamstress by her family.

• Beethoven handled the violin awkwardly and preferred playing his own compositions instead of improving his technique. His teacher called him hopeless.

• The parents of opera singer Enrico Caruso wanted him to be an engineer. His teacher said he had no voice and couldn't sing.

• Walt Disney was fired by a newspaper editor for lack of ideas. Walt Disney also went bankrupt several times before he built Disneyland.

• Inventor Thomas Edison's teachers said he was too stupid to learn anything. When Edison invented the light bulb, he tried over 2,000 experiments. A young reporter asked him how it felt to fail so many times. He said, "I never failed once. I invented the light bulb. It just happened to be a 2,000-step process."

• Albert Einstein did not speak until he was four years old and didn't read until he was seven. His teacher described him as "mentally slow, unsociable and adrift forever in his foolish dreams." He was expelled and was refused admittance to the Zurich polytechnic school.

• Louis Pasteur was only a mediocre pupil in undergraduate studies and ranked 15th out of 22 in chemistry.

• A total of 18 publishers turned down Richard Bach's 10,000-word story about a "soaring" seagull, *Jonathan Livingston Seagull,* before Macmillan finally published it in 1970. By 1975, it had sold more than 7,000,000 copies.

• When Lucille Ball began studying to be an actress in 1927, she was told by the head instructor of the John Murray Anderson Drama School, "Try any other profession."

• In 1952, Edmund Hillary attempted to climb Mount Everest, 29,000 feet straight up. A few weeks after his failed attempt, he spoke to a group in England. Hillary walked to the stage, made a fist, and pointed at a picture of the mountain, saying, "Mount Everest, you beat me the first time, but I'll beat you the next time because you've grown all you are going to grow . . . but I'm still growing!" On May 29, one year later, Edmund Hillary became the first man to climb Mount Everest.

Mark Victor Hansen and Jack Canfield are dynamic speakers and trainers on the development of human potential. They are the authors of the best-selling series *Chicken Soup for the Soul.*

25

Sacrifice the Queen

by Robert Fulghum

W*ithin my secret life* there are touchstones. Ideas, phrases, facts and notions I refer to time and time again—as often as I would consult a map when traveling. Among these treasures is a story from the world of chess.

During an international competition Frank Marshall made one of the most beautiful moves ever made on a chessboard. In a crucial game with a Russian master player, Marshall found his queen under serious attack. There were several avenues of escape, and since the queen is the most important offensive player, spectators assumed Marshall would observe convention and move his queen to safety.

Deep in thought, Marshall used all the time available to him to consider the board conditions. He picked up his queen—paused—and placed it down on the most illogical square of all. Marshall sacrificed his queen—an unthinkable move, to be made only in the most desperate circumstances.

Then the Russian, and the crowd, realized that Marshall had actually made a brilliant move. It was clear that no matter how the queen was taken, his opponent would soon be in a losing position. Seeing the inevitable defeat, the Russian conceded the game.

Marshall had achieved victory in a rare and daring fashion by sacrificing the queen. To me it's not important that he won. Not even important that he actually made the queen sacrifice move. What counts is that Marshall had suspended standard thinking long enough even to entertain the possibility of such a move. He had looked outside the traditional and orthodox patterns of play and had been willing to consider an imaginative risk on the basis of his judgment and his judgment alone. No matter how the game ended, Marshall was the ultimate winner.

On the checklist of operating instructions for my life this phrase appears: "Time to sacrifice the queen?" It turns up in unexpected situations.

Remember Tinkertoys?

Recall those interconnecting wooden parts—spools and rods—that came in tall canisters? Several years ago, when I taught art at the Lakeside School in Seattle, I used Tinkertoys in a test at the beginning of a term. I wanted to know something about the creative instincts of my students. On a Monday I'd put a small set of Tinkertoys in front of each student, and give a brief and ambiguous assignment: "Make something out of the Tinkertoys. You have 45 minutes today—and 45 minutes each day for the rest of the week."

A few students were hesitant to plunge in at first. The task seemed frivolous. They waited to see what the rest of the class would do. Several others checked the instructions and made something according to one of the sample model plans provided. Another group built something out of their own imaginations.

Almost always at least one student would break free of the constraints of the set and incorporate pencils, paper clips, string, notebook paper and any other object lying around the art studio.

I rejoiced at the presence of such a student. Here was an exceptionally creative mind at work. He had something to teach me. His presence meant that I had an unexpected teaching assistant in class whose creativity would infect other students. I thought of him and other such students as "queen sacrificers." They had "Q-S."

Sometimes one should consider crossing the line of convention. One need not be in a classroom or playing chess. Whenever life becomes a game of Tinkertoys, the queen may be sacrificed.

Robert Fulghum is a writer, speaker and painter. He is the author of the best-seller *All I Really Need to Know I Learned in Kindergarten.*

26

From Work to Home

by Jennifer James

I*t's the end* of the work day, and you're dragging your feet. You don't want to go home. You are tempted to hang around work, to run errands, maybe stop for a drink—to put off that moment when you pull into the driveway or arrive at the front door.

Perhaps you feel that things are unfinished at work. And since you don't want to leave them behind, you fill your arms or briefcase with bits of the office to take home. You know you probably won't work on it. But you deny yourself a transition to a place of comfort and pleasure. You have these feelings, even though you love whoever might be waiting for you at home.

Single men and women have the same feelings. The temptation is to keep on working because it's a familiar and comfortable pattern, or work to avoid being alone with yourself or the effort of setting up a social life.

Single parents or any parents sometimes dread the chaos they expect to find. Children create problems, demands and work that you have less control over than any you face on the job. They take over your energy when it's at a low ebb. Whether you live alone, are a homemaker, or you and your spouse both work, it's important to understand transition tension.

In his book, *Thank God It's Monday,* Pierre Mornell describes the transition problem. "Work and love are almost always opposites. Work is head. Love is heart. Work is rational. Love is irrational. Work is thinking. Love is feeling. Work is mask on and defenses up. Love is mask off and defenses down.

Work involves discipline and logic. Love requires play, passion and an absence of logic."

Making the transition from work to home or from home to connection with a loved one takes a little time.

What Works for You?

Check out the things you now do between home and work or just after you get home that might be attempts at transition time (reading, television, music, exercise, errands, cleaning, changing clothes, a drink, and so on). Most of us have an unconscious ritual for both leaving for work in the morning and returning home at night. Figure out what you're now doing.

Does it work for you? Which parts of the ritual help you to shift gears and give you a feeling of balance? What might work even better? Try now to imagine the perfect transition. Recognize your need for a transition and talk it over with whomever you share your home. Make conscious the ways you shift gears between work and home. Talk about your needs for privacy and quiet. Listen to the expression of the others' needs. Agree on strategies and compromises to meet both your needs.

Transitions involve cooperation. Consider transition time as a means to more intimacy. Minimize passive ways of tuning out. Maximize active transitions. Active transitions are activities, discussions or rituals. Passive ones are hiding, deferring, avoiding, not talking, drinking, or sleeping. If you can leave work in an active frame of mind, you can usually enter the transition to home the same way. You are deciding what you want to do instead of feeling that you have no choice.

Reconnect to your body by exercising after work or going for a walk. Stop and catch the sunset. Stop in a church and say a prayer. Picture the face of whoever might be at home waiting for you. Imagine the best place to be in your home relaxing. Make a joke about the day that helps you to let it go.

Use your imagination to shift gears so you don't deny yourself an evening of enjoying the comfort and love at home.

Jennifer James is a popular columnist, commentator, author, and speaker. She consults with organizations on various human development and relationship issues.

27

Against All Odds

by Les Brown

W*e all go through* hard times. There have been periods in my life when my car was repossessed, the power to my house was shut off, and nobody believed my dream. Don't accept those times in life when it seems the harder you work, the deeper the hole you dig for yourself. You've got to dig down deeply within yourself and make a gut check. Whatever is pushing you down right now, you have to say, "I'm going to make it no matter what!"

Believing in yourself requires knowing that your life has value. No matter what your circumstances are, there is a reason for you still being here. How can you begin to believe in yourself more?

1. Get positive encouragement from others. Make it a point to be around people who make you feel good about yourself, whether friends, family, co-workers, or mentors such as teachers and coaches.

2. Give yourself internal encouragement. Concentrate on saying things and doing volunteer work, working out, taking a class, listening to music or motivational tapes, reading inspirational books—anything that makes you feel good about yourself. Get in the habit of saying positive things to yourself.

3. Make deposits in a positive memory bank of achievement or good things you have done with your life. Savor your victories and achievements and moments of joy. Store them away for the hard times so that they can provide light in the darkness and hope when it seems like there is none.

4. Give yourself a break. Too many people blame themselves for hard times, when often they're part of a down cycle. We all go through those cycles in our lives. Don't assume responsibility for matters that are out of your control.

5. Grant yourself permission to make mistakes now and then, realizing we are God's, not gods. Even hard times in your life are the result of your actions; you should not condemn yourself. Has there ever been a life free of mistakes? So, take responsibility, take time to contemplate where you went wrong, and then accept that you are not perfect. Learn from your mistakes, make a commitment to change, then move on.

6. Put together a book or other positive reference source to lift you up. I call my version of this my Spirit Book because I go to it when I need my spirits lifted. It has pictures of my friends and family members enjoying life with me. It reminds me that hard times don't last forever, and that better times are ahead.

7. Get busy on smaller steps that take you toward your dream. Do not overlook the need to have small victories. Take victories wherever you can find them, whether from cookies that come out of the oven just right, or a 15-minute exercise program that leaves you feeling exhilarated. One step at a time, day by day. Stay in pursuit of your dreams and goals.

8. Resolve to replace worry with work, and avoid the idle mind when you are vulnerable. What is ever accomplished by worrying about what might happen? People who fret and worry and chew their nails waste too much time. Focus on solutions, not problems, and the way will become clear.

9. Look your best. Your appearance reflects how you see yourself and attracts the sort of people you want to attract. I don't know how people can expect to feel good on the inside when they look like 30 miles of dirt road on the outside. When you are feeling down, dress as though you feel like a million dollars. If nothing else, people will wonder what you are up to.

Les Brown is a renowned public speaker, author, and television personality. He was selected as one of "America's Top Five Speakers" by Toastmasters International.

28

Balance Your Life

by Marjorie Blanchard

While most of us recognize the need for balance in our lives, few of us know how to achieve and maintain that balance. Perhaps that's why looking at our lives through a model can be so beneficial. The model I discuss here was developed from two different studies: one dealing with peak periods of happiness, and the other with the effect of stress upon health.

1. Peak periods of happiness. When was the happiest period of time in your life? When did you feel that life was the most fun? the most meaningful? the most alive? Where were you? What were you doing? Who were you with? These questions have been important to me ever since I read of the research done by Herb Shepard at the National Training Laboratories. Herb asked people to think back to a period of several weeks or months when life seemed truly worth living. As they shared these wonderful times with him, he began to notice that there were common elements in the lives of these people.

2. The impact of stress. In the study on stress, researchers found that 80 percent of the people who experience several stressful events over time will develop a physical illness such as diabetes, ulcers, cancer or heart disease. Some other researchers have taken a different tack in looking at all this stress data. They have asked the questions: Why did 20 percent of these highly stressed individuals not get sick? What is happening in their lives that enables them to remain stress resistant or psychologically hardy? Interviews with people who survive 12 months of intense stress without becoming seriously ill reveal that they, too, share some things in common.

The similarity of the results confirmed my feelings that a simple model for life balance and satisfaction would help me and others to better manage the day-to-day options and demands of life.

The PACT Model

For convenience, I'll refer to these four elements—Perspective, Autonomy, Connectedness and Tone—as the PACT model of life balance.

Perspective. Perspective may be defined as seeing the big picture of life. People with perspective know their purpose and direction in life, value their past experiences, and have a keen sense of the present moment. Perspective is that broad picture of where you've been and where you're going that sets the context for this moment and for today. It may be strongly related to spiritual values. An example of perspective for me has always been Viktor Frankl, a World War II concentration camp survivor who wrote the book *Man's Search for Meaning*. Frankl observed that in this most degrading situation some people managed to keep going, while others seemed to lose their will to continue. One day they would refuse to get out of bed, and two weeks later they would be dead.

He observed that the people who kept going were those who had a purpose in their lives that they could hang on to: a great love they wanted to return to or work they felt compelled to finish—or a strong spiritual direction, even a strong desire to get by, day by day, and help others through the dreadful experience.

For each of us, perspective can translate into goals we want to achieve, values we want our lives to reflect, a sense of living each moment and day as if it might be our last.

Some of us have a very good idea of our professional goals and direction, but think little about our personal lives. For others, it's just the opposite. We do well at home, but our career or our career goals are uncertain or unclear. The challenge is keeping a balance between work and home that allows us to obtain goals in both worlds.

Autonomy. Autonomy is a feeling of control people have over their lives. People with a high sense of autonomy usually have a clear sense of their own identity, feel the freedom to make choices in their lives, have career or job options, possess good professional skills, and see their daily activities as moving them toward their goals.

Clearly, most people can't go through life in complete control of everything—and certainly a young mother with two toddlers and little money for babysitters has a different degree of autonomy than the mother whose youngest child has just entered first grade.

Again, people often have different degrees of autonomy at home and at work. At the office, they set goals, have meetings, have performance reviews, and progress well. At home, however, they never exercise; they break appointments with themselves and other family members; and they fail to develop skills in time management, parenting, and human relations.

Connectedness. Connectedness relates to the quality of relationships in people's lives. People who report high connectedness often feel they have positive relationships with friends, family, self, co-workers and supervisors. Connectedness also relates to a feeling of contentment and resonance with the physical environment. You can have a highly connected experience watching a beautiful sunset or walking into a home that you've decorated.

All relationships you have affect your connectedness, but the most important relationships are those with your spouse and your boss. In fact, the number one predictor of health at work is your relationship with your boss: a bad relationship can make people sick, while a good relationship can enhance a feeling of overall well-being and productivity. On the home front, are you spending quality time with your spouse? Do you make special efforts to plan "memory building" times together? Do you spend the time that you need to nourish the important relationships in your life?

Tone. Tone refers to how you feel about yourself physically, including the way you look, your health and energy level, your sense of fitness, even wardrobe and makeup. People with high tone generally have high energy levels, maintain proper weights, have sound nutrition, and feel good about their physical appearances. In their stories of peak periods of happiness, men very often talk about a time when they were active, looked good, had an abundance of energy, and were in touch with their physical selves. Over the years, I've found that when everything else seems to be floundering and I feel my balance slipping, the fastest and easiest element to work on is tone because you can see and measure results more quickly.

Balancing the Elements

The aim in life is to keep the elements of perspective, autonomy, connectedness and tone in dynamic balance. For example, when someone becomes ill or injured or hospitalized, their physical health (tone) is low. So we send this person a card or flowers to help him or her connect better to a sterile hospital room. What might the card say? "We care about you (connectedness). This won't last forever (perspective). Soon you'll be up and about (tone) doing what you want to do (autonomy)."

As you personalize the PACT model, it can help you even more. I use this model to keep my own life in balance and monitor the times when balance isn't present. If I notice I'm not looking forward to a given day or time or feel my energy is lagging, I try to step back and ask myself: "What's out of balance? Am I overcommitted or overstressed because I'm doing what everyone else wants me to do today without any time for myself? Or am I upset about a relationship with someone close to me? Or does my house feel untidy with lots of undone tasks—and thus doesn't provide a nourishing harbor from the stormy world? Or have I lost track of what all my efforts are for? Or am I confused about why I'm working 12 hours today and worked 12 hours yesterday and am not having time to see the people I love?"

The PACT model can help you pay more attention to life when you are feeling great and identify what's wrong when you feel out of balance.

Marjorie Blanchard is co-author of *Working Well* and author of *Satisfaction Guaranteed: Strategies for Managing a Complicated Life.*

29

Decry Decadence

by William Bennett

The *United States* ranks at or near the top in rates of abortions, divorces, unwed births, murder, rape, and violent crime. And in elementary and secondary education, we are at or near the bottom in achievement scores.

These facts alone indicate social regression. But there are other signs of decay—the moral, spiritual and aesthetic character and habits of our society—what the ancient Greeks referred to as its *ethos*. Here, too, we face serious problems. There is a coarseness, a callousness, a cynicism, a banality, and a vulgarity to our time—too many signs of civilization gone rotten. And the worst of it has to do with our children. At times, our culture seems dedicated to the corruption of the young, to assuring the premature loss of their innocence.

I worry that people are not angry enough. We have become inured to the cultural rot that is setting in. We are experiencing atrocity overload, losing our capacity for shock, disgust, and outrage.

The real crisis of our time is spiritual, or what the ancients called *acedia*. Acedia is the sin of sloth. But acedia is not laziness about life's affairs, but an aversion to and a negation of spiritual things. Acedia is spiritual torpor; an absence of zeal for divine things. And it brings with it, according to the ancients, "a sadness, a sorrow of the world." Acedia manifests itself in man's "joyless, ill-tempered, and self-seeking rejection of the nobility of the children of God." The slothful man hates the spiritual, and he wants to be free of its demands.

What afflicts us, then, is a corruption of the heart, a turning away in the soul. Our aspirations, our affections, and our desires are turned toward the wrong things.

So, What Can Be Done?

Only when we turn our desires toward the right things—toward enduring, noble, spiritual things—will things get better. Specifically, I suggest the following four things.

1. Recognize that we place too much hope in politics. Politics is a great adventure; it is important, but its proper place in our lives has been greatly exaggerated. Politics has too often become the graven image of our time.

2. Champion public policies that make the connection between our deepest beliefs and our legislative agenda. Do we believe, for example, that man is a spiritual being with a potential for individual nobility and moral responsibility? When we teach sex-education courses to teen-agers, do we treat them as if they are animals in heat? Or, do we treat them as children of God?

3. Recover a sense of the fundamental purpose of education. This purpose is to provide for the intellectual and moral education of the young. Having departed from this time-honored belief, we are now reaping the whirlwind.

4. Return religion to its proper place. Religion, after all, provides us with moral bearings. And if the chief problem we face is spiritual impoverishment, then the solution depends, finally, on spiritual renewal. The enervation of strong religious beliefs has demoralized society. We ignore religion and its lessons at our peril. But instead of according religion its proper place, much of society ridicules and disdains it, and mocks those who are serious about their faith.

Remember: it is a mistake to treat religion merely as a useful means to worldly ends. Although we are pilgrims and sojourners and wanderers in this world, ultimately we are citizens of the City of God—a City which man did not build and cannot destroy, a City where there is no sadness, where the sorrows of the world find no haven, and where there is peace the world cannot give.

William J. Bennett is the former United States Secretary of Education and the author of *The Book of Virtues.*

30

Forgive and Move On

by Desmond Tutu

Without memory, there is no healing. Without forgiveness, there is no future. It is not enough to say "let bygones be bygones." Indeed, just saying that ensures it will not be so. Reconciliation does not come easy. Believing it does will ensure that it will never be. Ultimately you discover that without forgiveness, there is no future.

To pursue the path of healing, we need to remember what we have endured. But we must not simply pass on the violence of that experience through the pursuit of punishment. We seek to do justice to the suffering without perpetuating the hatred aroused. We think of this as restorative justice.

We recognize that the past can't be remade through punishment. Instead, since we know memories will persist for a long time, we aim to acknowledge those memories. Restorative justice is focused on restoring the personhood that is damaged or lost.

But restoring that sense of self means restoring memory—a recognition that what happened to you actually happened. That acknowledgment is crucial if healing is to happen.

Denial doesn't work. It can never lead to forgiveness and reconciliation. Amnesia is no solution. If we are to be healed, we must come to grips with the past.

Vengeance destroys those it claims and those who become intoxicated with it. We live in a moral universe after all. What's right matters. What's wrong matters. You may keep things hidden, but they don't disappear. They impregnate the atmosphere.

If there has been continual fighting, even the smiles that are put on for you won't fool you. And so the pain must be addressed. We aim to remember, to forgive and to go on, with full recognition of how fragile the threads of community are.

Archbishop Desmond Tutu won the 1984 Nobel Peace Prize for his work against apartheid.

31

Real Progress

by Aleksandr Solzhenitsyn

Technological progress is marching on magnificently, but has led to three unforeseen and undesired consequences.

First, unlimited progress cannot occur within the limited resources of our planet: nature needs to be supported rather than conquered. We are successfully eating up the environment allotted to us.

Second, human nature has not become gentler with progress, as promised, because we have forgotten the human soul. We have allowed our wants to grow unchecked, and are now at a loss where to direct them. And with the obliging assistance of commercial enterprises, newer and newer wants are concocted, some of them wholly artificial; and we chase after them en masse, but find no fulfillment. And we never shall.

Third, the endless accumulation of possessions will not bring fulfillment. Possessions must be subordinated to other, higher principles so that they must have spiritual justification, a mission; otherwise, they become the tools of avarice and oppression.

Crisis of Soul

From this spasmodic pace of techno-centric progress, from the oceans of superficial information and cheap spectacles, the human soul does not grow, but instead grows more shallow, and spiritual life is only reduced. Our culture, accordingly, grows poorer and dimmer no matter how it tries to drown out its decline by the din of empty novelties. As creature comforts continue to improve for the average person, so spiritual development grows stagnant. Surfeit brings with it a nagging sadness of the heart, as we sense that the whirlpool of pleasures does not bring satisfaction, and that before long, it may suffocate us.

No, all hope cannot be pinned on science, technology, economic growth. The victory of technological civilization has also instilled a spiritual insecurity in us. Its gifts enrich, but enslave us as well. All is interests—we must not neglect our interests—all is a struggle for material things; but an inner voice tells us that we have lost something pure, elevated, and fragile. We have ceased to see the purpose.

Let us admit, even if in a whisper and only to ourselves: In this bustle of life at breakneck speed—what are we living for?

Gifts and Trials

It is up to us to stop seeing progress (which cannot be stopped by anyone or anything) as a stream of unlimited blessings, and to view it rather as a gift from on high, sent down for an extremely intricate trial of our free will.

The gifts of the telephone and the television, for instance, when used without moderation, have fragmented the wholeness of our time, jerking us from the natural flow of our lives. We must not simply lose ourselves in the mechanical flow of process, but strive to harness it in the interests of the human spirit; we must not become the mere playthings of progress, but rather we must seek or expand ways of directing its might toward the perpetration of good.

Progress was understood to be a shining and unswerving vector, but it turned out to be a complex and twisted curve that has once more brought us back to the very same eternal questions that have loomed in earlier times—except that facing these questions then was easier for a less distracted, less connected people.

We have lost the harmony with which we were created, the internal harmony between our spiritual and physical being, we have lost that clarity of spirit that was ours when the concept of Good and Evil had yet to become a subject of ridicule, shoved aside by the principle of fifty-fifty.

And nothing speaks more of the current helplessness of our spirit, of our intellectual disarray, than the loss of a clear and calm attitude toward death. The greater his well-being, the deeper cuts the chilling fear of death into the soul of modern man.

Having refused to recognize the unchanging Higher Power above us, we have filled that space with personal imperatives, and suddenly life becomes a harrowing prospect indeed.

The Cure: Self-limitation

The time is urgently upon us to limit our wants. It is difficult to bring ourselves to sacrifice and self-denial, because in public and private life we have long since dropped the golden key of self-restraint to the ocean floor.

But self-limitation is the fundamental and wisest aim of a man who has obtained his freedom. It is also the surest path toward its attainment. We must not wait for external events to press harshly upon us or even topple us; we must take a conciliatory stance, and through prudent self-restraint learn to accept the inevitable course of events. Only our conscience, and those close to us, knows how we deviate from this rule in our personal lives.

And yet, if we do not learn to limit firmly our desires and demands, to subordinate our interests to moral criteria, we will simply be torn apart as the worst aspects of human nature bare their teeth.

Today, self-limitation appears to us as something wholly unacceptable, constraining, even repulsive. Today, not many will readily accept this principle for themselves. However, in the increasingly complex circumstances of our modernity, to limit ourselves is the only true path of preservation for us all. And it helps bring back the awareness of a whole and Higher Authority above us—and the altogether forgotten sense of humility before this entity.

There can be only one true progress: the sum total of the spiritual progress of each individual, of the degree of self-perfection in the course of their lives.

Aleksandr Solzhenitsyn is the author of *The Gulag Archipelago*. This article is adapted from his essay that appeared in *At Century's End: Great Minds Reflect On Our Times*.

32

Active Faith

by Ralph Reed

Religious conservatives are not seeking to win government goodies or curry favor with politicians. They are reluctant political actors. After two generations of self-imposed retreat from political involvement, they have reentered the political arena with a common purpose and an uncommon enthusiasm. They look out upon a society they see as torn asunder by explicit sex and violence on television, rampant divorce, skyrocketing illegitimacy, epidemics of crime and drugs, and teen pregnancies. Their way of life and their values are under assault. For these activists, the most important issues are the family, a loss of values, a decline in civility, and the destruction of our children.

America today is struggling against forces as dangerous as any military foe it has ever faced. The threats, however, come not from without but from within. Families are disintegrating; fathers are abandoning their children; abortion is the most common medical procedure; and young people attend schools that are unsafe and in which they do not learn. In the inner city, illegitimacy is rampant; drug deals are openly conducted on street corners; hopelessness is the norm; and children are shot by marauding carloads of gang members. There is no economic solution to this social chaos—moral problems require moral solutions.

The pro-family movement grows and prospers by addressing these problems. Our solutions are so morally compelling that we can no longer be denied our place in the conversation. We shall experience triumph and disappointment, victory and defeat, leaps of progress followed by frustrating setbacks, but we will not be denied what is right.

Faith to me is not an ideology but a way of life. God's motives are higher than ours, and His message of love and redemption transcends politics.

Religious conservatives do not claim to have all the answers, but we do think we have identified many of the problems: illegitimacy, family breakup, cultural decay, illiteracy, crime, violence, and a poverty of spirit. We are people of faith struggling to do what is right, nothing more. We are sometimes wrong. As Lincoln observed during the Civil War, "While I know that God is always on the side of right and that He hates injustice, I am less concerned about whether God is on our side than I am that we be found on His." This is the proper perspective of faith in politics: fiery conviction of right and wrong tempered by humility before God and respect for one's foes.

Ralph Reed is former Executive Director of the Christian Coalition and the author of *Active Faith*.

33

Healthy Optimism

by Harold H. Bloomfield and Robert K. Cooper

As painful as disappointments and failures may be, they can be a potent force for positive change—but only when we learn to perceive them through the window of hope.

Few of us yet realize how much there is to be gained from cultivating an attitude of healthy optimism.

All healthy people periodically experience the "blues"—short-term dips in mood that last for a few minutes, hours, or even a day or two. And nearly all of us face periods of deep and abiding grief at the loss of a parent, spouse, or child or some other tragic life event—and sometimes this anguish takes many months to pass.

But overall, the mental attitude or outlook that pays the greatest dividends is characterized by flexible, real-life optimism or hopefulness that prompts you to be contemplative and sensitive to the world's needs on the one hand and active on the other.

Optimism can help make us more resilient under stress, heighten our vantage points, and help protect us against certain diseases. In contrast, pessimism makes a sense of helplessness and poor health more likely.

Flexible optimists usually have one eye on reality. They don't talk about how wonderful things are when, in truth, they're bad. Some men and women try to smile in the face of tragedies and difficulties and declare loud and clear that if everyone would just "be positive," everything will turn out grand. But in such cases, things do not turn out grand, because the big problems—when ignored—spread, and the small problems have a way of turning into big problems, too. And then things can really get out of hand.

Seven Positive-Minded Practices

We urge you to cultivate positive practices.

• ***Listen to yourself.*** When describing hassles, hurts, and difficulties in your life, what thoughts or statements do you use? One way your mind affects health is through explanatory style: the way you describe your difficult experiences to yourself and others.

People with negative explanatory styles tend to explain the bad things that happen to them in terms that are internal ("It's all my fault."), stable ("It's going to last forever."), and global ("It's going to spoil everything I do."). These individuals often exhibit learned helplessness and may be at greater risk for depression, repeated mistakes, and illness.

To look at a mistake and say, "It was just one of those things" and to realize that it's unlikely to be a problem tomorrow enables you to retain generally optimistic expectations for the future.

• ***Challenge negative thoughts.*** Pay closer attention to the way you explain mistakes and unpleasant situations to yourself and others—and start catching distorted, pessimistic thoughts. When possible, replace them with more constructive attributions. Be specific, honest, and constructive.

• ***Reward yourself for reaching small goals.*** As you reach each objective for a brighter attitude, reinforce your progress with rewards that you enjoy—perhaps going to a movie, reading a novel, going out for a special dinner, or buying a new piece of clothing you've been wanting for a while.

• ***Build your optimism in one life area at a time.*** Start with one aspect of your life where you find yourself feeling pessimistic. For example, you might begin by focusing on a strained family relationship or a difficult area of your work where you'd like to increase your hopefulness and optimism.

• ***Gain a measure of inner peace with forgiveness.*** There are times in all of our lives when another person has truly—and sometimes deliberately—wronged us. Unfortunately, in some situations, asserting yourself is not going to help—there is little chance that anything you can do will change what has been done to you. Although the event is over, you still find yourself remembering it, feeling the hurt, the anger, the bitterness, the rage and a desire to lash out. When this happens, it makes good health sense to release your angry thoughts and feelings by forgiving this man or woman who wronged you. Acknowledge that what this person did was wrong and choose to forgive him or her. Imagine yourself wiping a slate clean. Major wrongs—sexual molestation or rape, desertion by a parent or spouse, or any kind of violent crime—almost always require help from a qualified counselor in a safe, supportive environment where you can express your deepest feelings and work toward genuine, lasting forgiveness.

• ***Enjoy humor, as laughter can be the best medicine.*** A good laugh can lift your mind and mood—and perhaps even give a healthy boost to your immune system. In fact, lightheartedness and humor are vital to flexible optimism. In part, this is because humor can be a good defense against regret and perfectionism. And, since so much of our pessimism and anger is either petty or useless or unjustified, far too many of us miss golden chances to laugh at ourselves.

Laughter softens harsh judgments and helps us more readily accept our less-than-perfect selves. So find more moments to enjoy a good laugh.

• ***Use lessons of the heart to make sense of bad events.*** While optimism is associated with a state of vigor under stress, there are many events in life that we can't control or change. Sometimes when loss and pain are severe, optimism can be completely at odds with reality. In these situations, some people become despondent, hopeless, depressed, and ill. Yet in the same circumstances, other people continue to cope by accommodating themselves to the uncontrollable event or tragedy. They may ask, "Why did this happen? Why did it happen to me? How can this experience make me stronger or wiser or more compassionate or more tolerant or grateful for each moment from now on?"

Harold H. Bloomfield, M.D., and Robert K. Cooper are co-authors of *The Power of 5.*

34

Productive Aging

by Katharine Graham

I'*m learning that* productive aging means coming to grips with four challenging issues:

1. A general weakening of our mental and physical faculties. Whoever said age is only for the brave got it right. For instance, loss of memory—or, more precisely, retrieval—is a problem we all face. Sometimes a name will come back to you after a few minutes, and sometimes it doesn't. You learn to cover up and hope no one notices, or at least pretend they don't.

2. What to do with our time. You have to be involved in something that makes you want to spring out of bed in the morning. This doesn't happen automatically. You have to plan for it. Paradoxically, you can't face old age when you're old. You have to face it when you're young. Unfortunately, one of life's strange syndromes is that when you're young, it never occurs to you that someday you'll eventually be old.

Unless you lead a life of physical and mental activity from the beginning—with a diversity of interests—it's hard to suddenly change and acquire a new outlook at age 75.

I think the most important thing is to acquire a love of learning when you're a child, and to keep it all your life. It's wise to think about retirement well in advance, too. In your active years, you can't concentrate only on your work. You also have to care about your family. You have to develop outside interests.

If you live only for work, when the inevitable day of retirement comes, you die on the vine. Workaholics have a real problem. Their jobs are not only their obsessions, but also their identities—

particularly if they're high up in government, business, labor, or the arts. I think it helps to withdraw from the work force gradually.

3. Remaining objective about aging issues, such as mandatory retirement, social security, and Medicare. We're part of a big and powerful group. People over 65 are the fastest growing segment in the country. We account for more than 12 percent, and by the year 2025, the elderly will be up to 20 percent.

We must figure out how a smaller group of young people can help support the larger, aging population. Elderly people have an important voice in how these issues are resolved. We vote. So, we look beyond our own self-interest to what's good for the country as a whole, long term. For instance, people who depend on Medicare think adjusting the system means the end of the world. But if we don't do something, as we all know, the system will go bankrupt.

4. Thinking in terms of finality, sometimes philosophically, sometimes practically. We've come to realize the actuarial tables are not going to make an exception in our case. And we hope we can make a final exit painlessly, with grace, style, and dignity.

Be determined to achieve mentally and physically—above all, don't whine, be a bore, or feel sorry for yourself. And, of course, keep your sense of humor.

We have to try to keep growing and to keep learning, to keep our minds open, and to be sensitive to, and part of, the extraordinary changes taking place in the world.

Katharine Graham is the chairman of the Executive Committee, The Washington Post Company.

35

Power of Faith

by George Carey

The greatest challenges facing world order and peace will not be met without the motivating power of faith. How else can momentum be found for combating the worst excesses of poverty and inequality? How else can we find the self-restraint in the interest of future generations to save the environment? How else can we combat the malignant power of exclusive nationalism and racism? All this requires dynamic power of commitment, faith, and love. The privatized morality of "what works for me" will not do.

Some fundamentals of Christianity go to the very heart of reconciliation. It is posited on a purpose and power beyond ourselves: the tyranny of "me and my perspective" is broken. Christianity insists on justice, because we have a common Creator who loves every person equally. It teaches that we are all fallible and in need of God's grace, and this should undermine the pride which makes it difficult to compromise or say we're sorry. Our God of forgiveness encourages us to forgive those who sin against us. Those elements of reconciliation underpin so many initiatives in pursuit of justice and peace.

Four Simple Messages

What messages come as we feel the longing in the human family for peace? Let me suggest four principles.

1. Make room for others. Article 18 of the Universal Declaration of Human Rights declares: "Everyone has the right to freedom of thought, conscience, and religion. This includes the freedom to change his religion or belief." I call this the commitment to reciprocity. And we must not be half-hearted about it. Muslims, Hindus, Sikhs and others have equal rights to worship freely in the West and to make disciples just as Christians do. However, this must apply equally to the rights that Christians should have in places where they are in the minority.

2. Make tolerance central to your beliefs. Tolerance appears to be in short supply these days. But believers who deny it to others are denying something central to their religious tradition. In all mainstream faiths, tolerance and acceptance of differences are written into codes. Sadly, the injunctions to respect, honor, and tolerate those of other faiths are not always heeded. Terrible things continue to be done in the name of religion that shame religion and make it a disgrace. We need to ask: "Is it not time to espouse a genuine toleration which goes beyond mere acceptance of one another?" True tolerance has something to do with intensity of commitment towards another.

Indifference is often confused with tolerance. Baroness Wootton once observed sarcastically: "People are only tolerant about things they don't really care about." But genuine tolerance goes beyond indifference; it travels further than mere co-existence. It ends in risky identification with those whose faiths and lifestyles are different and with a commitment to living and working with them. We need to point to good examples which may provide encouragement and hope in a world damaged by indifference and intolerance.

3. Make room for common action and protest. Resist anything that is done in the name of religion which denies the true ends of religion. I think of extremism which ends in murder and violence. When acts perpetrated by fundamentalists occur, I am saddened by the fact that few leaders in such communities condemn the atrocities. There can be no justifications for acts that leave innocent people dead and wounded. People should not hide behind religious faith to justify acts of terrorism. Jean Kirkpatrick quotes a deeply religious Muslim who remarked: "Please do not call them Muslim fundamentalists. They do not represent a more fundamental version of Islam. They are simply Muslims who are also violent political extremists." Such extremists, wherever they are found, must not find a refuge in religious faith. True religion does not justify such behavior.

We can join in common action against racism, violence, and intolerance. We can be seen as communities of trust and sometimes as arbiters where disputes scar dialogue.

4. Hold the tension between the particular and the universal. We need never be apologetic about the universal claims and integrity of Christian faith or about mushy religious-sounding vagueness. I do not believe that all religions are the same, nor do I believe that Jesus Christ is merely one great religious figure among others. But, missionary faiths like Christianity and Islam have a duty to look carefully at the tension between making disciples, on the one hand, and respect for other faiths on the other. I believe the task can be done on the basis that faith claims are essentially invitations—invitations to consider that what our experience has meant to us may be something that may transform someone else. That implies that I, too, am obliged to listen to someone else's journey of faith and study the challenge that it brings to me.

In spite of the unique claims of faith communities, we must also note the impressive common ground we all share. On the eve of a new millennium, we desperately need to concentrate on what unites us. We owe it to our children and their children to build a more just and peaceful world, a world of tolerance in which love and harmony flower.

We need to go deeper into the traditions of our faith and be prepared to study other faiths more positively than we have done. As we do, we shall note that all the great human values that mean so much to us—belief in a purpose beyond ourselves, tolerance, justice, human dignity, love of others, respect for the elderly, the young and the vulnerable—are in fact universal religious values. The sacred texts of all religions represent the striving of the human heart for peace. They argue for solidarity and harmony among all people. "Love thy neighbor as thyself" is Jesus's summary of the Law. The same sentiment is to be found in all faiths.

George Carey is the Archbishop of Canterbury.

36

Bouncing Back

by Joan Rivers

I've survived everything—and I mean everything—and you can too! As painful as your challenges may be, they can teach you about your strengths, about who you are and what you value. Armed with that knowledge, you will reach a point where you will want to drop all grudges.

Yes, revenge is still sweet, but soon it goes sour. After a while, you have to let go.

The losses of all the people I've loved have made me try even harder to let people who are still alive know how much I value them. My mother's death was a poignant reminder to always tell people exactly what they mean to me. I will not let warm feelings go unspoken. We are all much stronger than we think. One night when I was laughing with friends, I suddenly realized that every one of us had taken blows that we'd thought would finish us; and yet all of us had not only survived but were laughing now. The human spirit is like one of those trick birthday candles: It simply cannot be extinguished.

In life the only thing that you can expect is the unexpected; the only surprise is a day that has none. I am always amused by those annual planners, in which people delude themselves into thinking that they are controlling the future. Only one entry will always be right: To be knocked on my butt and get up.

In the years since Edgar's death, I have rebuilt a life for myself full of challenge and purpose. Although I still miss him deeply and am grateful for the time we had together, the love we shared, and the daughter we raised, I am truly happy again.

And so, I will raise my demure little voice to tell you: With laughter and courage, you can survive anything and bounce back—and I mean anything. Just be honest with yourself about what you have lost, what you want from life, and how you're changing. Seek help when you need it and comfort when you want it. Don't judge yourself too harshly, and don't let anyone else's judgment stand in your way.

I wish you luck. More than that, I wish you the vision to create your own luck. In the design of your new life, may you be Frank Lloyd Wright. Remember: Everyone has a right to be happy.

Joan Rivers is a popular comedian and television personality, and the author of *Bouncing Back*.

37

I Think I Can

by Steve Young

In many ways, I'm not a likely candidate to be a quarterback in the National Football League. For starters, I harbored a lot of self-doubt for several years. In fact, it was only after being named MVP of the NFL a couple of years ago that I thought, "Hey, I'm pretty good at this."

For years, I was like The Little Train That Couldn't. I kept saying, "I can't do it. I can't do it." So the secret to my success is just that I held on. I knew I had the ability—deep down. But it seemed like success happened to me. I didn't happen to it. I sat there in a 3-D game, and it kept coming at me. I just kept going ahead, kept improving my game, and somehow never stopped. I just took it a day at a time. And over time, I became The Little Train That Could. My new message to myself is "I think I can. I think I can."

I overcame my doubts by learning to focus. I can be really uptight and worried before a game, but then all of a sudden, I lock in and perform.

Sports were never the central focus in my family. In fact, I didn't know my father played college football until I went to school. I think it's criminal what some parents today do to their children in the name of sports. If sports is anything more than having fun, it can be damaging to kids.

Thankfully, my father didn't lay out any rules, so I sort of learned to use my own initiative. As a result, I achieved things because I didn't want to disappoint him. To my father's credit, he never let football cloud his career vision, and that attitude rubbed off on me. When I finally started playing football professionally, I decided to use the time between seasons to go to law school. Each class, each professor and each book touched a different part of my personality. The education helped round me out.

Today I enjoy different aspects of life. I also read a lot of books. The more I know, the better I feel about myself. I want to be sure I have the preparation to do whatever I might want to do when I'm done with football. Reading helps me put my life in context.

I like to have associations and relationships that are as normal as possible. I make sure that people aren't put off—that the first thing on their minds isn't what money I have. I like to put my money where I can see it do some good.

Expectations are now very high. I liken it to when you first drive 55 on the highway. You think you're going 100 miles an hour. That's how I felt when I first started in San Francisco, trying to keep up with the legend of Joe Montana and the history of the 49ers. It seemed impossible.

I just started running as fast as I could. In time, I got used to the speed and expectations. Now I drive 100 miles an hour, but it doesn't seem fast.

I enjoy the team dynamics of football. There's no other place where you can take 11 very different men, put your heads together in a huddle and go out and do what you planned. There's immediate reaction, immediate scrutiny—not quarterly reports. It's played on a very basic level. You either get it done, or get off the field.

I've learned a lot about leadership and management through football. Management is how not to lose; leadership is how to go out and win.

Three Basic Principles

What has happened with me and the 49ers can happen anywhere because the common thread is leadership and coaching tied to three very basic principles of success:

• ***The first is ultimate accountability.*** At the end of the season if we haven't been successful, the owner turns to himself and asks, "What didn't I do?" If there's accountability at every level with every person, then there's no finger-pointing. If you allow finger-pointing, you self-destruct. I've been on teams where no one would take any blame for anything. You can't be successful that way.

• ***Second is having the basic tools to get the job done.*** I'm preparing myself for the day when my football career is over. I want to qualify myself. Whether it's reading books and educating myself informally, or getting my education at a university, I want to be as prepared and qualified as I possibly can.

• ***The third principle is simply moving forward.*** Somehow you get things done that you never thought you could when you just move forward. State your goals over and over, and soon they become realities. That's all I did. If I'm to be remembered for anything in football, it would be that I held on. The hardest part was having to wait behind Joe Montana. When I finally got my chance, the scrutiny was intense. I faced incredible odds. But I was drawn to that challenge. I kept saying, "I'm sticking this one out. I want to see where it goes." And one day I woke up as MVP of the league.

I'm an advocate of continuous education. You can always learn something. You can always make things work better. You can make a difference in some people's lives. I'm going to continue to climb mountains and meet new challenges. When I'm in my grave, I want my headstone to read, "Here lies Steve Young, who did this, this, and this. Oh, by the way, he also played football."

Steve Young is quarterback for the San Francisco 49ers and two-time MVP of the National Football League.

SECTION 4

Developing Your Career

38

Stop Wasting Time

by Hyrum W. Smith

B*en Franklin said,* "Do you love life? Then do not squander time, for that's the stuff life is made of." Controlling your life means controlling your time, and controlling your time means controlling the events in your life.

Have you ever heard someone say, "I've lost control of my life? I'm out of control!" What they're really saying is, "I am no longer in control of the events that make up my life. I am reacting to events. I do what everybody else thinks I ought to do, when they think I ought to do it." Being out of control is a terrible feeling.

But who has total control over the events in his or her life? No one. So, the question is this: How much control do you have? Imagine a control continuum. On one side are events over which you have total control. The other side represents events over which you have absolutely no control. Everything in between is partially controlled.

What are some events over which you have no control? The sunrise. Certain illnesses. Tornadoes. Death. Your boss. The stock market. The outcome of the Super Bowl.

How We Respond

What is important is how we respond to uncontrollable events in our lives. Often the most realistic response is to adapt. Live with it. Roll with it. It makes no sense to get upset over things we can't control. We must either adapt or be perpetually stressed out.

I frequently ask people to describe how they feel inside when they face events they can't control. They invariably use words like *frustration, stress, anger,* and *fear.* What level of self-esteem is associated with these words? Obviously, it's low. It doesn't feel good to be out of control.

There are events, however, over which we can have total control. Think about it. What can you control? The list includes such things as the time when you get up, what you wear, how you react to somebody else's attitude, what you eat. What do these events have in common? You. The only thing you have absolute and total control over is you.

What words describe how you feel when you control the events that you are able to control? You may feel confident, happy, exhilarated, powerful, surprised. But, two words encompass all the feelings you get when you are in control: *inner peace.* Inner peace is having serenity, balance, and harmony in your life through the appropriate control of events. The objective of good time management is inner peace. So, stop thinking "time management" and start thinking "event control."

In many ways, we've been conditioned to believe certain things about ourselves and our environment. We need to erase two effects of this conditioning if we want inner peace. First, there are events we can't control, but we believe we can. We waste time trying to control or manipulate our spouses or employees or children; ultimately, what other people do is out of our control. And conversely, there are events we can control, but we believe we can't. Many people, for example, feel that they are locked into careers they don't like, but in reality this is usually self-imposed bondage.

We talk ourselves into believing we cannot control events that we really can control. We give up when our options are by no means exhausted.

Why do most of us have so much trouble accomplishing the things that mean the most to us in the long term? Why do we never seem to get around to those things that really matter? One answer is that we've unwittingly bought into two fallacies about time that prevent us from dealing effectively with the events in our lives.

The first fallacy is that we think we'll have more time at some future date than we do now. "I'll do that next week, next year, when the children are grown, or when I retire. I'll have more time then." The second fallacy is that we think we can somehow save time. The fact is, you have all the time there is. You just need to recognize that you don't always do those things that are most important to you.

Your Magic Three Hours

Let me ask you, What are you currently doing with the magic three hours? You're probably wondering what the magic three hours are. Well, the magic three hours for me come every day between 5:00 a.m. and 8:00 a.m. Your magic three hours might be between 8:00 p.m. and 11:00 p.m. or any three hours of the day. Whatever you choose as your magic three hours, they make up that block of time that is generally uninterrupted, when you can focus on things beyond the normal urgencies and activities of the day.

Out of this focus on the important but not necessarily urgent matters of your life should come not only a better sense of your life mission and a weekly plan but also a practical, prioritized task list for the day—a list that tells you which tasks you're going to finish first.

Now, making a prioritized daily task list is a waste of time if you don't follow it. Once you identify your values, set long-range and intermediate goals, and spend 10 to 15 minutes a day planning your daily activities. Then comes the real test. The choice is yours. You can settle for a continuation of the status quo (with all its frustrations and lack of control), or you can achieve the things in life you really want to achieve. It's up to you. The only real variable is something called character.

Character, simply stated, is doing what you say you will do. A more formal definition is: Character is the ability to carry out a worthy decision after the emotion of making that decision has passed.

I promise you this: If you identify your governing values, set goals, and make and act on a prioritized task list each day—you'll start feeling the effects of exerting greater control over the events in your life. You'll be more proactive and productive, and you'll feel better about yourself. With those rewards and reinforcements coming your way, you'll find it a lot easier to continue this commitment. And, because your daily actions are actually reflecting your most deeply held values, you will experience an increased measure of inner peace.

Hyrum W. Smith is co-chairman of FranklinCovey and author of *The 10 Natural Laws of Successful Time and Life Management.*

39

Career Chase

by Helen Harkness

T*oday, we are forced* to do for ourselves what in previous decades was determined by our culture. We must come up with our own system to seek meaning and make sense of our lives.

Myths, the stories that guide our lives, are problematic today. Our current paradigm of career success is based on a system that no longer exists; so, using these outdated myths only adds to the chaos and makes us feel abandoned.

A Dozen Deadly Myths

The following 12 myths can destroy your career if you follow them.

MYTH 1. ***Our current chaos and disorder is temporary—it will pass, and the good old days will return.*** The more things change, the more they become different. No economic quick fix will work. New ways of understanding the roots of change have to be developed. For decades, we will continue to live with instability. We must look for new forms of work and new approaches for self-help, and invent new services. We must train for the future, not the past, developing mind, not muscle; brainware, not hardware. The new worker will be more independent and resourceful.

MYTH 2. ***One life equals one career. The work we select, or somehow back into, is a lifetime commitment.*** One life equals one career is not an option. Getting beyond this myth will require us to push beyond outdated policies and systems, past cultural barriers and our own fears of failure and the unknown. Weathering the criticism and questioning of family and friends requires a creative plan built on self-knowledge and the changing environment. This is the ultimate in creativity—the redesigning of our career based on our needs. Multiple careers are a reality for all of us.

MYTH 3. ***Old dogs can't learn new tricks.*** In midlife or advanced age, we can launch into the most creative and productive time of our lives! The key to thriving in today's world at any age is learning, unlearning, and relearning. Learning "new tricks" is a continuous process for people who are open to new ideas and who welcome opportunities to grow and change. They engage in genuine self-renewal and growth; develop flexibility and diverse identities across their life spans.

MYTH 4. ***Increasing middle-class affluence and expanding opportunities are our inherent right.*** Rising expectations and declining affluence are clashing head on! Surpassing the educational and financial achievements of our parents is a fundamental archetype, a major cornerstone of the American Dream. The development of alternative career paths and a new definition of career success is especially critical for the sons and daughters of those people who have achieved highly successful careers.

MYTH 5. ***Career success, happiness, and high self-esteem directly correlate with status, money, and upward mobility.*** There is no conclusive evidence that people who make the most money are happier or feel better about themselves! Finding one's meaning and mission may be the most critical step to happiness, however we define it. Mission, not money, motivates: Only purpose fights our fear of nothingness.

MYTH 6. ***Planning a career isn't necessary because someone or something will rescue and direct us.*** You are in charge of your career. No one is coming to rescue your career but you! If you are not in charge, no one is! If you don't know what you want or need for your success, no one does. If you don't have this wisdom, acquire it. That is what career planning is all about.

MYTH 7. ***Superior performance will be automatically recognized and rewarded.*** Superior performance and quality work should be respected and rewarded. But don't count on it unless you are willing to be disappointed. The best qualified people do not necessarily get the best jobs or the most money unless they have a keen awareness of how these things happen in their workplace.

MYTH 8. ***A college degree is the key to a good job and career success: The more advanced the degree, the greater the guarantee.*** College degrees can't be counted on for getting a great job. Continued learning is an absolute essential! However, don't confuse learning with the acquisition of degrees. Formal education should be pursued with an understanding of its real value to us. It may not bear material rewards or upward mobility, but it can be a major force, reordering our priorities and providing a deeper knowledge of self, nature, and society.

MYTH 9. ***Select your career on labor market projections: Go where the best jobs and most money and security are predicted to be.*** To assure career satisfaction, select your career based on what fits your individual skills, interests, motivations, and values, and balance these with projected opportunities. Never base a career selection solely on the anticipated job market. If it isn't a match for you, success will be difficult for you to achieve and maintain, and you may never value your success or translate it into high self-esteem.

MYTH 10. ***Successful people make no mistakes.*** The road to success is checkered with failures, false starts, and frequently, grave mistakes. Addiction to perfectionism and fear of failure are deadly dictums to career success and creativity. If you spend most of your psychic energy concentrating on your weaknesses, you will neglect your strengths. You need to know your strengths—what you do well naturally—and focus on taking these skills to their highest level.

MYTH 11. ***Sacrificing your private life is the price of success; dropping out of the corporate world is career suicide.*** In the future, there will be few, if any, ladders up. There are multiple alternatives to career success. We can have it all, but not at the same time. Success in both personal and career life is a juggling act. To do this successfully we must identify, choose, and attend to our top priorities.

MYTH 12. ***There is only one right way to be, think, act, and succeed.*** You can choose from multiple, diverse, and wide-ranging ways of being, thinking, doing, and acting. Each of these can be valuable, effective, and right, depending on time, place, purpose, need, and other factors in life.

These 12 myths have the power to destroy our careers. Understanding them is essential to career control.

Helen Harkness is president and founder of Career Design Associates, Inc.

40

Hitting Stride

by Charles Garfield

The most productive people tend to be students all their lives. Discovering and developing new facets of their potential excite them the way mastery of a sport excites an athlete, particularly when mastery increases the speed at which improvements occur.

Peak performers often comment that regardless of past accomplishments—which in many cases are formidable—they know they are using but a small fraction of their capacities: "I am still developing and have a long way to go." "I'm starting to hit my stride now."

Four Potentials

From their observations I have distilled four main ingredients of the potential they have managed to mobilize:

1. Inherent talent. Inherent talent, an inborn predisposition, whether handed down from prior generations or not, is the wiring in one's system that is unique to each individual. One can either identify and develop the specific talents and capacities he or she has, or leave them buried. Peak performers find compelling reasons to cultivate relevant inherent talents. Matching a mission to such gifts greatly enhances the possibilities of peak performance. What often happens is that a vast reservoir of hidden resources becomes available for use.

2. Acquired information. Acquired information, the complex mass of skills and data about the world that was learned since the original wiring was set, may or may not be of much use. That depends on how much of it you can recall and use appropriately. Teachings you don't apply are not going to produce much. Insight is not equivalent to results, and people often do not act in their best interests even when they possess the knowledge they need. Acquired information, like inherent talent, may lie dormant until you develop an action plan and a compelling reason for using it.

*3. **Restlessness.*** Restlessness, an inner urge to apply one's talent and information, is not a learned skill. It is part of the "hard-wiring," the fixed circuitry that a human being comes with. Science writer Morton Hunt refers to "a capacity to find things interesting." What makes us want to know about something, even something of no practical value, such as the age of the universe or when human beings first appeared on earth? In *The Universe Within,* Hunt suggests it may be "an intrinsic characteristic of our nervous system, an inherent neurological restlessness, a need to do something with the thoughts in our minds and with the world they represent."

A baby in action—curious, energetic, reaching out to explore—embodies the inborn urge to grow, achieve, excel. This motivation need not be taught, but can be untaught, as organizations and limiting jobs show in squelching people's motivation. Peak performers prove that human beings are goal-seeking and meaning-seeking organisms. We are not only born in a state of arousal, excitation, and motivation, but we also seek to grow in a particular direction. What determines that direction?

*4. **Passion and preference.*** Preference with a passion—intense commitment to what they do—is one of the single most dramatic differences between peak performers and their less productive colleagues. High achievers differ in what they call it: passion, preference, deep feeling, commitment. They agree, though, that it determines their direction. Many told me they can trace their performance more clearly to preference than to aptitude, more to how they feel about what they are doing than what they know. One 44-year-old sales vice president in the automobile industry remarked, "So many of us are top-heavy with skills, information, and talent—mostly unused—and light on commitment. I can't help thinking of Oliver Wendell Holmes saying, 'Every calling is great when greatly pursued.'"

Having a calling greatly pursued—and, often enough, greatly achieved—does much to enhance one's self-esteem and self-confidence. Former Chrysler chairman Lee Iacocca and Vince Lombardi, the legendary coach of the Green Bay Packers, once had a conversation. Iacocca remembers Lombardi saying:

"Every time you go out to ply your trade, you've got to play from the ground up—from the soles of your feet right up to your head. Every inch of you has to play. Most important, you've got to play with your heart. If you play with a lot of head and a lot of heart, you're never going to come off the field second."

Peak performers start with potential. We all do. Yet history is littered with the bones of people who never converted potential into achievement. Inherent talents turn useful only when you cultivate them. Yes, training can be dull, tedious, and onerous. But when it serves a passion and follows a mission, it becomes a practice as pleasurable and full of promise as refining a golf swing or making a successful investment. Top performers do not leave training to chance. They focus carefully on what they need not just to survive but to excel, which is the surest way to survive.

Charles Garfield is CEO of the Charles Garfield Group and author of *Second to None* and *Peak Performers*.

41

Success in a New Job

by Clyde C. Lowstuter

Some roadblocks to your success are of your own making. These are rooted in what you believe to be true—your perceptions of reality. If you believe you are too old, you are. If you believe that there is no opportunity, there won't be.

When the search takes a long time, you may think, "I'll never get a job!" Rejection can batter your self-esteem. You may feel that the right job is eluding you, and that the odds are stacked against you. But, if you believe in yourself and deem yourself to be worthy, if you are committed to your success and trust your skills, you will find the strength and courage to go on.

Seven Keys to Success

The following seven steps are keys to boost your self-esteem and self-confidence in your professional pursuits.

1. Develop superior credentials. If you are currently employed, seek ways to strengthen your credentials by enhancing your knowledge, skills, and abilities. Look for competency gaps and fill them. Model success. Identify mentors. Go to them. Ask what specific behavior they engage in or thoughts they hold to be successful. Do what they do, think the affirming thoughts they think, and feel what they feel. Create a powerful résumé and attention-getting marketing letters that distinguish you from others.

2. Manage your emotions. Strive to create and manage those emotions that you desire—from being energized to being joyful, resourceful, confident, open, dynamic, bold, creative, innovative, and even wise. Visualize an event or a time in your life which captures that emotion you want to recreate easily—feeling confident, for example. Concentrate on a specific scene in which you were confident and zoom in on what you were doing, how you were moving and talking, gesturing, laughing, and smiling. As you recapture these empowered feelings, you can feel confident any time you choose.

3. Change how you think about things. How you attach to things will significantly influence how you feel about them. If you view something that has happened to you as incredibly unfair, then you will feel victimized and indignant about it. But if you view it as a learning experience, you will see opportunity for significant gain.

4. Learn, understand, and apply behavioral models. Models make real the abstract. If you incorporate behavioral models which empower you, you have the ability to make significant shifts in the way you think, feel, and act.

5. Identify and focus on your desired outcome. Determine what you want and need in your life and your career in specific terms. Goals such as wanting a better job, more money, less hassles, better relationships, and reduced stress are too general. Specific goals enable you to focus on the outcome. Once finely focused, your goals mobilize you into action.

6. Become committed to your success. The greater your commitment, the greater will be your resolve to let nothing stand in your way. Live by the adage "The extent to which you are committed to your success is the extent to which you will achieve it!"

7. Fine-tune your strategy, remain flexible, and pursue stretch goals. Not only do you need to know where you presently are and where you are headed, but you also need to adapt your behavior when you are off-track.

Pursue stretch goals worthy of your efforts—goals that challenge you to be the best you can be and provide a sense of accomplishment and fulfillment when you achieve them.

Success in Your New Job

Once you land a new job, here's what to do your first few months to be successful.

• *Learn how to contribute value.* If you don't feel you are adding value, then do some research to figure out how you can help.

• ***Identify those individuals whom your function impacts and meet them.*** Get to know their needs, interests, and motivations. Learn about their roles and responsibilities. It is critical to your own success that you know what works for your colleagues. Ask them, "If you could have anything you want from this position, what would it be? What are you willing to do to help make this function serve you better?"

• ***Gain support and endorsement of others (superiors, peers, and subordinates) by informing and involving them in your thoughts, feelings, ideas, and intentions.*** If you ask for their input, most people are pleased to support you. Involvement fosters commitment.

• ***Take care of the company, and the company will take care of you.*** Bring to the job a sense of urgency about the task at hand. Your professional future will basically rest with your performance reputation established within your first 18 months on the job. Repeatedly ask yourself, "What's needed and what's wanted on the job, in the company, in my relationship?" Don't be political. This can be permanently damaging. Therefore, refuse to discuss personalities or to take sides.

Know the Business

Know more about your business and company than you need to know. Ask about new products or new projects or programs. Learn how the company operates and become known to as many people as you can.

Always have a plan that you are working against and measure performance. Review monthly what you have done. Measure your own performance against your own goals. Give yourself a quarterly performance review. Be tough on yourself. Expect results, not perfection.

Keep things moving. Make things happen. Do not sit on yesterday's successes. Everything you do will have a direct positive or negative impact on the bottom line. Prudence dictates better performance.

Clyde C. Lowstuter is president and CEO of Robertson Lowstuter, Inc., a leading career and organizational development firm.

42

Retirement Reflections

by Warren Bennis

The word "retirement" does not have a very positive connotation; in fact, many people do not find it a particularly pleasant prospect. The old French word "retirer" is made up of the prefix "re," meaning "back," and the verb "tirer," meaning to withdraw, to take back, to retreat.

Aside from not being happy with the word "retirement," I'm not completely pleased with the euphemisms for retired people like "senior citizens" or "seasoned citizens."

Another reason for my discomfort is that retirement is a topic that is relatively new to me and new in my thinking. I've just begun to think about retirement and have tried to understand my resistance to the topic.

And, finally, having reached the age of 70, I've begun thinking, maybe it's denial. I guess I was jolted out of my denial when I was attending a conference in Monterey and somebody came up to me and said, "Didn't you used to be Warren Bennis?"

Two Basic Ideas

I wish to share two basic ideas. First, successful people are always in transition. These people never stop. They keep going on. They never think about past accomplishments, or about retiring.

I was once asked by a magazine writer, "Who are your heroes? Whom do you most respect regarding the aging phenomenon?" I rattled off the following names: Winston Churchill, Bertrand Russell, Clint Eastwood, Mel Torme, Colin

Powell, Bill Bradley, Grace Hopper and Kay Graham. I began thinking, "What do they all have in common?"

Well, they got off to late starts, but they just keep cresting, never coasting. I don't think they talk about retirement or past accomplishments. They're always redesigning, recomposing, and reinventing their own lives.

At some point in their lives, they stopped trying to prove themselves and began to express themselves. That transition is a very interesting one, one I'm not sure I've accomplished myself.

Second, people who have been successful in their careers and in life are also successful in all transitions. People who have not been very successful in their lives, in their careers, don't adjust well to any transition. And to them and to me, it's simply death on the installment plan.

My studies on outstanding leaders suggest that they share five characteristics that would bring about successful transitions, or successful "retirement." The first is a strong sense of purpose, a passion, a conviction, a sense of wanting to do something important to make a difference. Second, they are capable of developing and sustaining deep and trusting relationships. Third, they are purveyors of hope. Fourth, they seem to have a balance in their lives between work, power, and family or outside activities. They didn't tie up all of their self-esteem on their position. Fifth, they all have a bias toward action. They all are people who seem not to hesitate in taking risks, who while not reckless, are able to take action. They love adventure, risk and promise.

Warren Bennis is Distinguished Professor of Business Administration and Founding Chairman of the Leadership Institute at USC, and author of *Organizing Genius* and *Old Dogs Can (and Must) Learn New Tricks.*

43

The Creativity Quest

by James C. Christensen

I *spoke recently* with a woman who was showing my paintings and sculptures. She said, "You are so lucky to be blessed with an imagination. I have none at all." She then asked: "Where do you get your ideas?"

Her comments set me thinking. Where do I get my ideas? How does one "think up" things? Where does inspiration come from? I have never had a problem "thinking things up" and have, since childhood, had a very active imagination. But how does it work?

Many adults see imagination and creativity as something reserved for artists, writers, and other "creative" types. But I believe that everyone has the potential to be creative.

The Card Catalogue

As I thought how imagination works, I came up with the metaphor of a card catalogue in a library. When we are born, the catalogue is filled with mostly empty cards. Each card in the catalogue represents a single thought or idea stored in our minds. We fill out the cards through our six senses. Everything that we see, touch, hear, smell, taste, and sense through inspiration creates a card, or a set of cards. When we are children, we fill out cards like crazy! The world is a fascinating place, and we have no inhibitions about exploring, learning, and experiencing. We freely experiment with the ideas we are collecting, and make strange connections and unique leaps of logic.

We have an entire world of images, objects, and experiences to add to our catalogue. Firsthand experiences are best, strong and immediate. But with the explosion of technology of communication, we can also access places, cultures, images, and ideas that we might never experience firsthand. This gathering of information, this building of the card catalogue, is the first requisite of imagination. The bigger our card catalogue, the more potential for imaginative thinking we have.

The process of imagination is nothing more than the combining of "cards" in unique ways. Every "original" thought is based on information that we already have stored. Whether by a methodical process or by sheer serendipity, all new ideas come from the combination of existing concepts put together in ways that no one has ever done before.

What Kills Creativity?

So what slows us down?

Many people are stuck in "thinking ruts." As we grow up, we learn certain patterns of thought. We find solutions that work and which we repeat again and again. Some of these patterns are good and allow us to function. Many of the habits we have help us to get through the day efficiently. But unfortunately, too many of us, in the routine of our lives, allow too many thinking ruts to develop, and we lose the ability to get out of those ruts to find original solutions. As "life" takes over, our imaginations atrophy, like any muscle that is not exercised. After a while, many of us would echo the comment, "I don't have an imagination."

My response to you is "Yes, you do have an imagination. Yes, you do have the capacity to dream, to invent, to create, to "think things up"! You just need to exercise your imagination in the same way you exercise your muscles. And the more you exercise, the easier it becomes to be creative.

If you find yourself fishing out of the same bucket for ideas, perhaps it's time to find a bigger bucket, or at least put a few new fish in the bucket you have! So, read, travel, observe, walk, hike, have conversations with new people, make notes, listen, study, take advantage of every opportunity to add to your card catalogue. Don't just add more of the same stuff. Reach out for things that are less familiar, a little outside of your comfort zone.

Be willing to take a few risks and try new things and ideas. These new cards, collected firsthand or vicariously, will trigger new thoughts, sounds, and images and add to your creative potential.

Those ideas, sounds, rhythms, patterns, and images become inspiration, points of departure for creative work.

Sir Joshua Reynolds, the 18th Century English painter said, "It is indisputably evident that a great part of every man's life, must be employed in collecting materials for the exercise of genius. Invention, strictly speaking, is little more than a new combination of those images which have been previously gathered and deposited in the memory: nothing can come of nothing; he who has laid up no materials can produce no combinations."

Keep a Journal

So, be aware of what goes on around you. Document your experiences. Keep a journal or a scrapbook. When I travel, I make journal entries, along with sketches. These may never turn into paintings, but they help me to capture thoughts and impressions.

Often one idea leads to another. That is one of the fascinating things about the imagination. Many of the combinations won't work, and a lot of ideas are only important in that they lead to other ideas that eventually lead to something that might be significant.

Einstein said: "As one grows older, one sees the impossibility of imposing your will with brute force. But if you are patient, there may come a moment when, while eating an apple, the solution presents itself politely and says 'Here I am.' "

By "playing" with ideas and imagination, through art, or writing, or telling stories or playing games, or creative daydreaming, we increase our ability to "think things up."

We must be willing to experiment, to be comfortable with flights of fantasy and exploratory thinking. We must move out of our comfort zone into the unknown territory of "What if . . ."

We all have the ability to imagine. We all have the potential to extend our thinking limits, to get out of our thinking ruts, to create, as we are made in the image of the Creator.

James C. Christensen is a popular painter and illustrator. This article was adapted from a speech at Brigham Young University.

44

The Well of Creativity

by Mihaly Csikszentmihalyi

Creativity has to be a new idea that is valued and which is brought to fruition. That's creativity with a big C—creativity that changes the culture. We can talk also about personal creativity—creativity in the way you approach life, in the way that you experience life, with originality, openness, freshness. Creativity that makes life enjoyable, but does not necessarily result in fame or fortune.

Everybody can have creativity at the personal level and make his or her life more interesting and more like a process of discovery.

Although everyone can be creative, often we aren't because there's just so much market for new ideas or new ways of doing things. There's a tremendous inertia and conservatism in any culture. It has to be like that. We can't invent new things all the time. We are conservative by nature. We like the same food. We like the same traditions. To some extent, we need tradition and security, but then we also need creativity.

Often it's a synergy of forces, circumstances, and even luck that makes a person creative.

Many people who are very creative and well-known in their fields have said luck is what made them achieve what they did. By that, they meant that good genes are luck, having a background that allows you to focus on a particular domain of knowledge is luck, being at the right time and right place is luck.

Along with luck is perseverance. Many creative people cite their ability to hang in there during tough times. Whether you're a poet or sculptor or scientist or businessperson, your everyday work involves a small amount of wild, marvelous ideas and a lot of perseverance and hard work. Thomas Edison said: Creativity is one percent inspiration and 99 percent perspiration. I think it's true. You have to transform those wild ideas into something that will endure, and that's hard work.

When you're creative, you're not always dancing to someone else's tune. You develop your own rhythm of work and rest. During idle time, ideas have a chance to recombine in new ways, because if we think consciously about solving a problem or writing a book, then we are forcing our ideas to move in a lock step and straight line. Probably what comes out is not very new or original. For original ideas to come about, you have to let them percolate in a place where you have no way to make them obey your own desires or your own directions. So they find their way. Random combinations are those that are driven by forces we don't know about. Something new may come up, but not when we try to push ideas directly.

People who transform the domain in which they work have certain similarities in their personalities. They have what I call complexity of personality, which means that each one of us has several personality options. We can either be extroverts and enjoy people, but then feel anxious when we're alone. Or we can be introverted, which means that we like solitude but can't handle people.

In many other dimensions of personality, we are either masculine or feminine. Or we're cooperative or competitive. Creative people, I find, have the ability to use the full range of this separate dimension so that they have masculine and feminine traits. Both men and women have some of the strengths of the opposite gender. They can be introverted when they have to be, when they have to work. They love being alone and working, but they also love being with people so they can get the important information and know what other people in their field are thinking and doing.

Creative people are playful and responsible at the same time. Most of these people are both very rebellious and iconoclastic. They like to break rules; they like to break norms. But, they're also very traditional. Whatever they accomplish is based on the accomplishments of previous generations. They take those accomplishments very seriously, and yet they are willing to go beyond and break the limits of what has been done or known in the past. You have to be traditional, and you have to be iconoclastic. These polarities are somehow integrated in creative people's work.

They work not for the result of the work they're doing, or for fame. They work for the sheer joy and exhilaration of doing it. Motivation and curiosity are very tightly interwoven.

Most of us are very creative at holding ourselves back. As children we have creative experiences spontaneously. We have interest, curiosity, and excitement about life. Unfortunately, sooner or later, they're beaten or educated out of us. Schools, unfortunately, discourage curiosity and self-directed interest. Part of being creative is having a sense of wonder, a sense of awe at life. It would be nice if more people could feel that. We think that the little cubicle in which we live and the little routine that we learn is life. Then that's it. There's nothing interesting outside of that. That is a sad situation for those who live that way.

Creative people are divergent thinkers. They hold a diversity of ideas and explore many possibilities. Our education is based on convergence thinking, which is to point people toward the same solution, and the one "right" answer. Divergent thinkers start with something completely obvious, and they see a number of possibilities in it.

So, instead of converging on one right solution, you diverge through possibilities. One possibility may be very important and interesting. That's how you generate discoveries—by asking questions. Or whenever somebody tells you that something is so and so, say, "Well, let me think of it as being the opposite." Turn every statement into the opposite and see how it looks from that other 180 degrees reversed. Creativity is not in the answers, but in the questions we ask.

Better with Age

Creativity gets better as we age. People in their eighties and nineties have certain faculties declining. Their memories maybe aren't as good. They make some mistakes. But their creativity often improves over time.

One thing that surprises me is that many older people say that they are much more able to take risks. In the life of these people comes a time when they say, "Hey, don't have to worry as much about the opinion of my peers. I have already proven something. Now I can try something on the fringe and see whether it works or not." You still have to be self-critical. You still have to evaluate whether what you're doing makes sense or not, but you can run more risks.

There is a feeling, also, of moving into new areas or connecting between fields that seem disparate, but you begin to see similarities with experience and age. Many people feel that they're very satisfied by being involved in more social and political issues. So they expand the reach of their activities to move beyond a narrow specialization.

You often have to trick yourself into believing that "This is the voice of the muse; this is a story that I just have to tell." Then you make it through by working hard.

But sometimes it may not just be mental trickery, but it may also just be the drive from within that "I have to do this." It can come from a deeper level. The drive is there, but it's through hard work that this trivial idea becomes something beautiful. If you take it seriously and begin to put your effort and energy into it, then you can create a work that is awesome. But you can short-circuit that process if you know too much about the beginning, because then you think "It's already been done."

All of us can spend our lives doing what we love to do. We can all be creative. Each one of us can experience the feeling of discovery. We may not have the luck to occupy the niche of an Einstein, but we can certainly appreciate the mystery of the universe or the beauty and harmony of nature. All of those things we can learn about, we can participate in, we can enjoy, and at that level, creativity is what makes life full and worth living.

Mihaly Csikszentmihalyi is a professor of psychology and education at the University of Chicago. He is the author of many books including *Flow, The Evolving Self, Creativity* and *Being Adolescent.*

45

Your Life's Work

by Peter Senge

Learning is the enhancement of capacity to produce results that really matter to you. You're very inquisitive about things you really care about, and you need to tap that intrinsic motivation in your work. Because once you start coming to work to do your life's work, everything changes. When that connection develops between what really matters in your life and what you're doing professionally, work has a very different meaning.

If you find little meaning in your job, you may be doing something you really don't want to do. Are you able to do what you really want to do? Can you bring your whole self to work? If you look at successful people, you see in their eyes a belief that if you do something well and love to do it, money will be a natural by-product. For you to prosper over the long term, you must contribute something. And the more you can contribute on multiple dimensions, the more you're likely to prosper.

We're often so hooked on getting it right that we miss the essence of the creative orientation, which is to aspire to something worth our effort. You probably will never fully accomplish your vision because the vision is an abstraction. And, the more progress you make, the more you will see your inadequacy.

Creative tension occurs when we have a vision of where we want to be, we tell the truth about where we are now, and we notice that there's a gap between the two. Creative tension points us in two directions: toward our aspiration, but also toward our ability to inquire into the current reality—both conditions and causes.

Many people are disoriented. They don't know what they're supposed to be doing. They're wondering: "What is my role? What do I do now?" We need to think of ourselves as designers, stewards, teachers, and self-motivated people. The world has changed profoundly but we haven't changed with it. We've acquired awesome power to shape the world. And yet our wisdom hasn't increased. So, our work must really be about making a better world.

We need to figure out the nature of the wake-up call. It's not enough to be paralyzed by fear or apprehension. We have to have a better sense of what changes we are being called to make, and then make them.

Peter Senge is a faculty member of the Massachusetts Institute of Technology, director of the Center for Organizational Learning at MIT's Sloan School of Management, and author of *The Fifth Discipline.*

46

Boost Your Career

by Brian Tracy

I*magine that* it's possible for you to earn 10 times your current annual wage. If you're earning $25,000, imagine that it's possible for you to earn $250,000.

The tragedy is that while the main preoccupation of many people seems to be money, or the lack thereof, the average person has the potential to earn far more than he or she is doing currently.

Is the person earning $250,000 per year 10 times as smart as the person earning $25,000? Ten times as experienced? Does he or she work 10 times harder? Of course not. None of these is physically or mentally possible, but there are people in every business earning many times more than others with the same age, experience and intelligence.

It's not what you have but what you do with what you have that will determine your success or failure. Abraham Maslow, the great psychologist, said that the story of the human race is the story of people selling themselves short. Many people are spinning their wheels in careers where they should be moving rapidly onward and upward.

Here's how you can put your career on the fast track.

1. Choose your job or career with great care. The choice of a job or occupation for which you are ideally suited comes before anything else. If you try to work at something you don't enjoy or don't believe in, you'll never be happy, and you'll never be successful.

2. Become excellent at what you do. You have to pay any price, go any distance, spend any amount of time necessary to "be the best." Extraordinary rewards only go for extraordinary performance; average rewards for average performance. You are being paid today exactly what you're worth—no more, no less. If you want to earn more, you must increase your worth, your value.

Peter Drucker says that only the truly competent individual can be free of politics in an organization. When you're good at what you do, you can rise above politics. It's the mediocrities who have to play games and although they sometimes succeed in the short-term, they invariably fail when everyone figures them out. So pick your work carefully and if you don't love what you're doing enough to want to be the best at it, get out! Working at something you don't care about is the very best way to waste your life.

3. Next, work for the right company and the right boss. The right company is one that respects its people and practices pay for performance. The right company is dynamic, growing, open to new ideas, and full of opportunities for people with ambition.

Much of your happiness and job satisfaction depends upon your relationship with your superior. If you don't get along, make every effort to resolve it or get transferred but if you can't, be prepared to walk away.

Choosing the right work, the right place to do it and the right people to do it with is laying the foundation for career success.

4. Seek a strategic niche. Some jobs are more critical to the health of the organization than are others. A strategic niche is a job or position that influences the cash flow of the company. In most companies, cash flow is determined by sales and marketing, and if you want to get ahead rapidly in those companies, you must work your way into the sales and marketing function.

To increase your income, you must be in a position to increase revenues or cut costs. So look at your company and look for a niche where you can become more valuable.

5. Develop good work habits. It's the fastest way to bring yourself to the attention of your superiors. Most people are time wasters; they waste not only their own time but also that of others. And because of this, they have a hard time getting ahead.

If you develop a reputation for speed, dependability and quality work, you will immediately stand out from the majority. Two qualities mark a person for promotion: 1) the ability to set priorities, to separate the important from the unimportant, and 2) the habit of getting the job done fast, a sense of urgency. People who have a sense of urgency are always on the fast track.

6. Keep learning. High achievers in every area make a commitment to ongoing personal and professional development. They look upon themselves as self-made people, as works of art in progress.

Subscribe to book clubs and book summaries. Build your own library of important books in your field. Never be cheap about your education.

Listen to educational audio cassettes in your car. If you do nothing but use that traveling time as learning time, that alone could make you one of the best educated people of your generation.

Remember, to earn more, you must learn more. Your outer world of results will always correspond to your inner world of preparation. I've always loved the poem by Henry Wadsworth Longfellow: "The heights by great men reached and kept were not obtained by sudden flight, but they, while their companions slept, were toiling upward in the night."

7. Cultivate good relationships with others. Holding constant for knowledge, skill, luck and intelligence, your success will be in direct proportion to the number of people you know and who know you in a positive way. Your network of contacts and relationships can and will do more for your career than any other factor.

Successful people spend a good deal of time networking with others. So join your professional or trade association. Get involved with community affairs. Get out among other people whom it would be useful for you to know.

The more of yourself that you give away without direct expectation of return, the more will come back to you from sometimes the most unexpected sources.

Frederick Nietzche said that man can bear any "what" if he has a big enough "why." Why do you want to be a big success? If your reason is big enough and compelling enough, nothing will stop you from getting onto the fast track in your career.

Brian Tracy is a popular speaker and author of *Success Is a Journey.*

47

Character and Competence

by Norman Schwarzkopf

To be a 21st century leader, you must have two things: competence and character. I've met a lot of leaders who are very competent, but they lack character. And for every job they do well, they seek a reward in the form of promotions, awards, or decorations—in the form of getting ahead at the expense of somebody else or in the form of another piece of paper that awards them another degree. And the only reason they want the decoration is to secure a faster route to the top. These may be very competent people, but they lack character.

On the other hand, I've met many leaders who have superb character, but they aren't willing to hold their own feet to the fire; they aren't willing to pay the price of leadership. They are not willing to go the extra mile, to do the extra little bit. Those extras are what it takes to be a great leader.

Not Being Watched

I look for both character and competence. I would never send a leader who lacked one or both of these vital attributes into battle. Because when you lead in battle, you are leading people—you are leading human beings. A competent leader will stand in front of a platoon of 44 people and think of them as a platoon. But a great leader will stand in front of the same platoon and think of them as 44 individuals, each having hopes and aspirations and wanting to live and do a good job.

So, you must have competence, and you must have character. Some great man once said that character is best seen in men and women when nobody is watching them. It's not what people do when they are being watched that demonstrates character; it's what they do when they are not being watched that demonstrates true character. And that's what leadership is all about.

General Norman Schwartzkopf is a retired general of the U.S. Army. This is an excerpt of his address at West Point.

48

Zest in Your Work

by Andy Grove

Zest is inevitably present in people with high energy and drive. Small wonder, if you think about it: We spend most of our lives at work. It's certainly easier to sustain a high commitment if we enjoy our work. So, do everything you can to enjoy yourself at work. Just remember while you are having fun: it is a place to work! Here are six pointers:

1. Celebrate achievements. Provide interim milestones, and supplant the long-term drive toward reaching a major result with a series of shorter steps. Then when one of these is achieved, celebrate in some small way. Poke gentle fun at each other, including your boss. Keep internal competition light.

2. Rotate jobs. Even if you stay with one organization, rotate jobs occasionally. Any job can become tedious after a while. It is harder to create and sustain energy and drive if you have the same job forever. Working in different assignments keeps your work interesting and enriches your skills.

3. Enjoy the people you work with. Our co-workers are very important to us. They are a major factor in determining whether or not our work is pleasant, congenial, maybe fun. Problems with co-workers, even minor disruptions, can ruin our work. Handle co-worker problems directly. Confine the discussion to the specific complaint you have and avoid generalizations such as "you always this . . . and never that."

4. Enjoy your work. It is impossible to like all of it. Sometimes you will chafe under its unrelenting nature; other times you will be bored, but overall you must enjoy it. You will like your work if you can see that what you do makes a difference, and you approach your work with zest, maybe even playfulness. Doing so induces a bit of levity when it's most needed and leads to camaraderie.

5. Be dedicated to your work. Be dedicated to the end result, the output, not how you get to it or whose idea it is or whether you look good or not. Respect the work of all those who respect their own work.

6. Be straight with everyone. I hate it when people are not honest with me, and I would hate myself if I weren't straight with them. There are always many reasons or excuses to compromise. We may reason that people are not ready to hear the truth or the bad news. Those rationalizations usually lead to unethical conduct and backfire every time.

Andy Grove is CEO of Intel Corporation.

SECTION 5

Continuous Improvement

49

Total Fitness

by Jimmy Connors

W*e all need* to go beyond exercise to receive the gifts a healthy lifestyle has to offer and to contribute as long as possible. The concept of fitness isn't limited to how far you can run, how much weight you can lift, or how flexible you are. It is balancing all elements in your life: physical, mental, emotional, spiritual.

1. Physical fitness. You understand how important doing the right exercise is in relation to both the quality and length of your life. You realize that you probably don't need much exercise to receive great benefits and that a regular exercise program doesn't have to intrude on your lifestyle. It can and should complement all the other facets of your daily routine. I think my success as a 40-year-old professional tennis player proved that.

2. Mental fitness is about exercising your mind, being aware of what's happening in your neighborhood, your city, your state, your country, and the world. There are many ways of giving your mind a workout. I like reading the paper—not just the sports section. Books are another great source of information for me. They can take me to places I've only thought about (or only seen from a hotel room and tennis court) and make me feel as though I've been there.

I enjoy learning about what makes other people tick. Even if I don't agree with an opinion, it's good for me to listen and at least try to understand the reasoning behind it. I don't think I've ever met a person who couldn't teach me something.

My mother encouraged this curiosity in me as a small child. She saw to it that my life consisted of other things besides tennis. There was time set aside every day for homework and for playing with friends. She didn't want me to be one-dimensional or to believe that tennis was my only option.

My mom knew that if I made tennis my whole life, I'd get burnt out quickly. Instinctively, she knew that for me to get to the top and stay at the top, tennis would always have to be fun.

3. Emotional fitness. Physical activity is essential for keeping emotions in check. It allows us to blow off steam and clear our heads before saying or doing something we'll regret later. It also helps me to keep my mind on whatever I'm doing at the moment. This lesson was an important one for me.

Meeting and marrying my wife, Patti, was the best thing that ever happened to me. When I got married, I was at the height of my career. Patti knew and understood from the beginning what the sacrifices would be. That didn't make our lifestyle easy. We traveled from city to city and country to country, in and out of hotels one after another. A crowd of people was always around us. And when we were at home I spent a lot of time practicing. Although I was trying to build a foundation for our future, I had to take into consideration what she must have been feeling. I wanted her to know how much it meant to me to have her there.

I knew I had to make a change, and I did. What I did was discipline my emotions. I taught myself to concentrate on what I was doing at the time. When I was practicing, I practiced hard. I tried not to think about anything but the game when I was on the court. But when I was with the family, I was with them 100 percent. They had my undivided attention. This has worked for me. Now I have my family and friends, a business to run, and tennis. I've found the time for all of it.

If you are having trouble keeping your emotions in check, look at yourself the way I did. It is possible that you're trying to be in too many places at the same time. When that happens, everything suffers. We are entitled to feel every emotion; we just have to make them work to our benefit. There is no crime in taking time off from the job to relax and enjoy the things we work for. But if you're thinking about playing the whole time you're working and about working the whole time you're playing, you don't get much from either. If you can learn the value of keeping your mind on what's in front of you, you'll get more from both worlds.

I know many people who say they feel guilty about coming home to the family after a long day and heading straight for a workout. The best advice I can give you is to try to involve your family in exercise and make it something you can all do together. If that's not possible, sit down and talk to them about why exercise is so important—that it will keep you with them longer. If you can make them understand, they'll be upset if you don't work out. Exercise should be important not only to you but to all those you love and care about.

4. Spiritual fitness. I'm not talking about religion, although religion can certainly be included in this element. What I mean is being satisfied with the person you are on the inside. Nothing I've earned or done would mean anything to me if I didn't feel I had gotten it with integrity.

I'm not just Jimmy Connors the tennis pro anymore. I'm one-half of Mr. and Mrs. Connors and one-fourth of the Connors family. My kids depend on me to show them the way, the right way. Again, I owe this to my mom. She said a long time ago, "Jimbo, when you're on the court you can be a tiger. You fight for what you want and be proud of your efforts. Off the court, you're just like anyone else. You must respect women, set an example for your children, and earn your friendships. The only kind of man worth being is a gentleman." And she was right. I'm not only proud of the things I've accomplished, but how I've accomplished them.

The same can be true for you. While I'll be the first to say that exercise isn't everything, it will make your life richer in many ways. It can't take the place of loving relationships, although it can make them more fulfilling. It can't pay the mortgage, yet it can give you the energy you need to work harder. Exercise itself won't bring you more friends, but by relieving stress, it can make you friendlier. Exercise is a tool to be used and enjoyed in many ways and for many reasons.

Jimmy Connors has won eight grand-slam singles titles, 109 career singles titles, and has the record for holding the #1 ranking for more consecutive weeks than any player in the history of tennis.

50

Learn to Win

by Lou Tice

People with an optimistic view of their capabilities outperform those who are doubtful or simply more "realistic," even though their abilities are virtually identical. They don't give up easily or worry about obstacles because the final outcome is never in doubt—they see themselves as creative, resourceful problem solvers. They believe themselves into being more.

Why do some people see themselves as winners and act accordingly, while so many others don't?

Learning to Win

Learning to see yourself as a winner and to feel like a winner happens primarily as a result of having successful experiences and thinking self-affirming thoughts. When we believe our efforts will be successful, we become venturesome and are most likely to undertake an activity or task. Because we expect to succeed, we persist until we do. This successful experience causes self-affirming thoughts, which boost our self-esteem, enhance self-efficacy, make us feel good, and lead us to believe we will do well in the future. Thus, we attempt more, and the upward spiral continues. This internal system helps us grow and develop—a natural continuous quality improvement program.

There is, however, an equally powerful downward spiral that can interrupt the natural growth process. If we believe we are likely to fail, we undertake activities tentatively, expecting a negative outcome. We feel anxious about our performance, and we avoid or remove ourselves from anxiety-producing situations. When we fail, we say "I told you so" to ourselves and make a mental note to avoid similar situations in the future.

When we're very young, we have little to say about the experiences to which we're subjected or the messages we receive from the world. The authority figures in our lives often shape our early thoughts and feelings. If they abuse this power, we may be conditioned to believe that the world is not a friendly place, that we have to struggle to get our basic needs met, that we are not loved (lovable), valued (valuable) or competent. Years pass and the pattern repeats many times. It becomes part of who we are, imprinted in our brains, and our internal voice, our self-talk, takes on the sound of our harshest critics. We play out the negative conditioning without thinking about it.

Over the years, my work has brought me into close contact with many "winners." The common characteristic is not what, but how they think. Through a dazzling array of experiences, all of them have learned the importance of a clear vision and sense of purpose or mission. They have discovered that clearly envisioned and articulated goals speed their achievement of that purpose. They have developed tremendous resiliency, great faith in their abilities, and self-talk that constantly affirms their own value. They feel deeply connected to the world in which they live and fully accountable for their actions.

The best tools and the latest information won't help us tap into our rich potential until we accept that we are ultimately responsible for who we are, what we do, and who we become. This means that we give up looking for someone or something to blame and abandon the "victim mentality."

If we think of ourselves as losers or failures, we will do what we can to make sure "reality" supports our view. Even positive deviation from that picture makes us uncomfortable, producing anxiety and a desire to "get back to where we belong."

But if our picture of reality is that we deal with obstacles well and persist until we succeed, we will do whatever it takes to make that picture match the world. We will seek challenge, enlist help, solve problems creatively, and refuse to quit until we have met our goal.

Mentoring Others to Greatness

Most successful people have benefited from a relationship with someone who served as a mentor to them.

Three factors make a mentor credible to us: 1) the mentor is like us in a significant way; 2) he or she has achieved a measure of personal success in a relevant field; and 3) he or she has mentored or coached others to success in that field.

We can hold up the most admirable models, the highest quality benchmarks, and we can say to our children or to our employees, "Here, look at this, and be like this." But if they can't see themselves being and doing those things, if the pictures we hold up or the examples we set aren't assimilated, no lasting change will result.

Who have your best mentors been and what have they done for you? I'll bet that they were people who could see more in you than you could see yourself. They saw you not only as you were, but also as you could be. They didn't focus on your mistakes and shortcomings. Rather, they described to you, frequently and vividly, your strength, power, and potential. Because they were credible, you gave sanction to their vision. Over time, you developed a new internal standard. You said, "Yes, that's me. I am like that." And you acted accordingly.

People naturally move in the direction of praise—and away from harsh, devaluing criticism. If someone tries to motivate you by making you afraid of what will happen if you don't do something or by continually pointing out your flaws, faults, and mistakes, you will allow them to influence you only as long as you have no other choice. At your earliest chance, you'll be out of there. Long before you make your escape, though, your subconscious will help you get away by coming up with creative "reasons" why you can't perform, including injuries and illness.

When you emerge from a mentoring relationship, you have enhanced self-esteem and self-efficacy. You also feel deeply humble and grateful. But you do not believe the credit for your growth and gains belongs entirely to your mentor. You recognize that what was achieved under your mentor's tutelage and guidance was your own doing.

Lou Tice is chairman of The Pacific Institute and author of *Smart Talk for Achieving Your Potential* and *Personal Coaching for Results.*

51

Dynamics of Winning

by Denis Waitley

What separates the real superstars from those who have fleeting success? My response to this question is given in a series of 12 messages.

1. The drive to win. The making of a champion begins with a burning desire for change. Winners are grateful for who they are, but dissatisfied with the "status quo." The drive to win is the first step in long-term high achievement and success: Motivation springs from within the champion; it is not pumped in, pep talked, or sparked from external sources. By definition, motivation means "motive in action" and a motive is that obsession which drives from inside to external manifestation.

2. Paying the price. Winners willingly do things the rest of the population would never consider trying. Paying the price means focusing on developing the skills and training regimen of champions—observation, imitation, repetition, and the internalization of skills into habits and reflex actions; also, learning why and how to go the extra mile and seeing success as a marathon, not as a dash.

3. The Olympian within. Winners believe in their worth in advance of their performance. Most people base their worth on their current status or achievement, which means that until they are judged successful by society's standards, they have little to be proud of. Champions believe in their dreams when they have only a dream to hang on to, even in the face of criticism and superior achievements by others.

4. Fame, fortune and integrity. Champions who win consistently have an uncompromising attitude about self-honesty. They respect honesty, they try to base their decisions and actions on the truth, and they constantly strive for new knowledge and truth. They all seem to function according to an "integrity triangle" consisting of three basic questions: 1) Are my beliefs based on truth? 2) Do my words and actions correspond with truth and honesty? 3) Before I speak or act, do I honestly consider the impact of my decisions on other people and the environment?

5. The visualization of victory. The mind has a marvelous capacity to engage in "instant preplay," as well as "instant replay," of future and past performances. In sports science, this guided imagery or visual-motor rehearsal is one of the key factors that constitute the winner's edge. Masters use the mind to simulate championship performances. Learn how to live in your imagination, since visualization plus internalization equals realization; how to create mental holograms of excellence.

6. Stress without distress. Convert stress into power and energy. The ability to remain calm, to maintain composure under pressure, and to perform at your very best during the intense heat of competition is the mark of a champion. Many talented individuals perform well in practice and in familiar arenas; however, they "choke," "tighten up" or lose their cool when the chips are down and everything is on the line.

7. Getting in "the zone." For the champion, there is a unique experience that occurs moments before and during the ultimate performance. It is one of total concentration, in which all critical senses are heightened and all distractions are filtered out. It is called "the zone." Focus is completely on the desired result in the present tense. The past and future do not exist when you are performing in "the zone" in sports, business and personal life.

8. Strength through mental toughness. Champions hang in there when the going gets tough. They take enormous setbacks and failures in stride and come back to win again and again. Steve Young, Dave Dravecky, Babe Zaharias, Glenn Cunningham, Wilma Rudolph and Pancho Segura are just a few of the winners who have come from behind and overcome. Champions view failures as learning experiences or temporary inconveniences or interruptions on their road to success, and will tolerate little distraction from pursuing their ultimate goals.

9. The "coachability" factor. Champions are always open to alternatives and new input to improve their performance. Consistent winners are not the arrogant, spoiled egotists who dominate the media spotlight with their tantrums, antics, and feelings of superiority. The most successful individuals in the game of life are most often the most humble, most approachable, most gracious and grateful, most agreeable and non-judgmental with others and most critical of their own performances, as well as most eager to learn and improve.

10. Being a team player. A team in harmony is synergy in motion, where the whole is greater than the sum of the individual talents. When all assignments are understood, when each takes 100 percent of the responsibility for doing his best and when individual egos are subordinated for the benefit of the team—a quantum leap in performance takes place. Learn how to become interdependent, without sacrificing individuality; how to stand out while "fitting in"; how to gain the respect and trust of others; how to put others on your own success team.

11. The quality of leadership. Great teams, great companies, great families and great countries always have great leaders. Real leadership is the process of empowering others by abdicating one's power over them. It means to set others free to become all they can be in an atmosphere of inspiration, innovation and mutual respect. Learn how to inspire greatness in those around you; how to lead naturally and spontaneously.

12. Beyond the arena. The real challenge in the game of life is to maintain balance and harmony while excelling in one area or professional endeavor. After the season is over, the champion must change into street clothes and become a parent, companion, spouse, citizen and neighbor. The greatest mark of the authentic champion is the way he or she relates to society beyond the arena or stadium and translates superb performance in one, specialized field into a "global perspective" to benefit this and future generations.

Denis Waitley is chairman of Denis Waitley, Inc., and the best-selling author of *The New Dynamics of Winning* and *The Psychology of Winning for Women.*

52

Toughness Training

by James Loehr

The painful shock waves of change and growth inflict wounds on the human spirit. People feel numb, confused, afraid, exhausted, suspicious, empty, overwhelmed.

Change is necessary, of course. Waste and redundancy have forced us to reengineer and resize. But failing to factor in the impact of change on the human spirit is a tragic mistake.

Sport teaches us a powerful lesson: remove heart and soul from the performance equation, and maximum output becomes an unattainable fantasy.

There has never been a greater need for personal renewal. To maintain high levels of performance, you have to possess remarkable mental, emotional and physical toughness. In effect, you must become a corporate athlete by deepening your capacity for tolerating stress; increasing your ability to perform at high levels regardless of circumstances; and enhancing your personal health and happiness.

Toughness Training is a way of thinking, acting, and living that raises your performance to new heights. A core concept is the balance between energy expenditure (stress) and energy recapture (recovery). World-class stress requires world-class recovery if maximum productivity and health are to be maintained over time.

Five Strategies

Here are five strategies to help you perform better:

1. Face the truth. Honestly answer these questions: How much stress can you take mentally, physically, and emotionally?

Are you tough enough to handle current life demands? Are you performing to the upper level of your potential? Can you handle that level of stress without compromising your personal health or happiness? What are your recovery skills? What are your weaknesses, and what are the costs of those weaknesses? Are you fully engaged emotionally? To what extent does your spirit need to be revived?

2. Improve your Ideal Performance State (IPS). When you are confident, relaxed, energized, positive, calm, challenged, and fearless, you perform at your best. When you are not tough enough to handle the stress, or when your spirit has been ravaged from too many nonstop battles, your talent and skill become frozen in time.

The right feelings and emotions free and empower us; the wrong ones trap and defeat us. Emotions and feelings are body talk reflecting the balance of stress and recovery at any given time. Positive emotional states and empowering states such as enthusiasm, passion, motivation, and challenge reflect stress-recovery balance. Negative emotional states and disempowering feelings such as helplessness, depression, fatigue, and fearfulness reflect imbalance. The first step in improving your IPS is awareness: tuning into the connection between feeling states and performance levels, between empowering feelings and stress-recovery balance, and between feelings and physiology.

3. Improve your acting skills. What distinguishes an Academy Award winner, a Wimbledon champion, or an Olympic gold medalist from the rest of the competition? It's the person's ability to trigger genuine emotion on demand.

How we look and act leads to changes in how we feel. Emotional states have measurable physical characteristics. And nowhere is your emotional state more closely reflected than in your face. Developing a discipline for how you look and act under stress helps you control negative arousal so that you avoid the feelings of fear, frustration, and failure that cause despair, defeat, and disaster.

Top performers project powerful images when they perform under stress. How you walk, how you carry your head and shoulders, and the expression on your face can stimulate emotion-specific responses. Going through the motions gets the emotions moving in that direction. Looking calm, challenged, energetic, and confident in a stressful situation has a very positive effect on performance.

4. Become a stress-seeker. By deliberately seeking stress, you increase your functional capacity. Often stress is impossible to avoid and difficult to reduce. But you can learn to deal with it, to win out over it, even to be nourished by it. You can use normal life stress to toughen yourself, particularly during periods of crisis and adversity. Tough times represent opportunities for getting tougher.

Deliberately increasing the volume of stress in your life—by exercising, by taking on new challenges and added responsibilities—is an indispensable part of the training process.

When you are tougher physically, you get tougher mentally and emotionally. These three realms—mental, emotional, and physical—are so intimately connected that when you impact one, you influence the other two. That's why exercise is so critical.

5. Train your mechanisms of recovery. Anything that seriously compromises the personal health and happiness of an athlete, whether on or off the playing field, will eventually have disastrous performance consequences. Sleeping habits, eating habits, drinking habits, relaxation time, the volume of active and passive rest, naps, and even fun become serious training considerations.

You don't have personal coaches to help you establish consistency in your sleep habits, the frequency and timing of your meals, and your recovery time. So, you simply have to become your own coach. You must train your mechanisms of recovery to world-class levels.

Your career is 30 to 40 years. Talk about endurance! Upholding high productivity day after day demands great stress-recovery balance. Learning how and when to recover for maximum benefit, learning how to recover quickly, and learning how to build recovery into your everyday schedule are important in all three arenas: productivity, health, and happiness.

James Loehr is an internationally acclaimed sport psychologist, author of *Toughness Training,* and founder of LGE Sport Science, Inc.

53

Whole Person Health

by Rachel Naomi Remen

I'*m not at all* certain the mind is the highest human function. Or perhaps the mind is the highest human function—but we transcend our humanness. Something in us participates in our humanness, but has its source and its connection far beyond it, and in that connection may lie the hope of healing.

When people talk about mind-body health, they tend to deny spirit or even to omit it totally. The term *mind-body health* suggests gaining mental control of physical functions or fixing the body by using the mind. This idea appeals to many people, because the mind is a simpler, safer, cheaper, more efficient, more affordable way of fixing the body than, let's say, surgery.

But health is not an end. Health is a means. Health enables us to serve a purpose in life, but it is not the purpose in life. How we live is not as important to me as why we live. Why are we here in these bodies? What are we doing here like this? So the real questions of health may not be questions of mechanism but questions of spirit. At the very heart of spirit is mystery. And the problem with the mind is that the mind cannot tolerate mystery. The mind denies that which it can't understand, and we are a mentally identified culture. In valuing the mind as much as we do, we tend to deny mystery, to deny the spiritual.

What Is the Spiritual?

It's much easier to say what isn't spiritual. The spiritual is often confused with the moral, but it's not the moral. Morality is concerned with issues of right and wrong, and reflects a social tradition or consensus. What is considered moral varies from culture to culture and from time to time. Morality often serves as the basis for judgment, for one group of people separating themselves from other groups, or individuals separating themselves from others. Yet the spiritual is profoundly non-judgmental and non-separative.

The spiritual is also different from the ethical, which defines the right way to relate to other people, to carry out business and to behave in general. If the moral is not the spiritual, then the ethical isn't either.

The spiritual is also not the psychic. The psychic is a capacity we all share, although it is better developed in some than in others. It is a way of perceiving. We may use a psychic power to know the spiritual—but that which we know is different from the means by which we know it.

I can use any of my senses to impress others, to accumulate personal power, to dominate or manipulate—in short to assert my separateness and my personal power. The spiritual, however, is not separative. A deep sense of the spiritual leads one to trust not one's own lonely power but the great flow or pattern manifested in all life, including our own. We become not manipulators but witnesses.

Lastly, the spiritual is not the religious. A religion is a dogma, a set of beliefs about the spiritual, and a set of practices which arise out of those beliefs. There are many religions, and they tend to be mutually exclusive. Yet the spiritual is inclusive. Perhaps one might say that the spiritual is that realm of human experience which religion attempts to connect us to through dogma and practice. Sometimes it succeeds and sometimes it fails. Religion is a bridge to the spiritual—but the spiritual lies beyond all religions. The most important thing in defining spirit is the recognition that spirit is an essential need of human nature. There is something in all of us that seeks the spiritual. This yearning varies in strength from person to person, but it is always there in everyone. And so, healing becomes possible. Yet there is a cultural tendency to deny the spiritual—to delegate it at best, to ignore it at worst.

We tend to delegate the spiritual to others who are more interested in it, or who we feel are perhaps better equipped to deal with it. In reality, of course, the spiritual can't be delegated. We all participate in it. It is our very nature, the core of our humanity. There is no situation that is not a spiritual situation; there is no decision that is not a spiritual decision; there is no feeling that is not a spiritual feeling. In fact, the very essence of life may be spiritual in nature. Life advances a spiritual agenda that we all work toward together, without even knowing it.

The Purpose of Life

Some people who are dying seem to arrive at a sense of what life's purpose is, and it is not to be a doctor or to be well-known or even to make a social contribution. The purpose of life, as these people tell it, is simpler: to grow in wisdom and to learn to love better. If life serves these purposes, then health serves them and illness serves them as well, because illness is part of life.

Denying the spiritual is bad for your health. Much illness may have its roots in unrecognized spiritual distress—issues of isolation, of anger, the feelings people have that they don't matter or that nobody matters to them. I think that depression is not so much an issue of nobody loving you. Depression is an issue of not being able to find a place to give your love, not being able to love enough.

What we call stress might really be spiritual isolation. It might really be an insensitivity to and a lack of recognition of our spiritual needs. And so they are unmet, largely because they are unrecognized. What is spiritual isolation? Basically it is living with a closed heart.

A human being is not a mechanism, but an opportunity for the Infinite to manifest. The only thing really worthy of our study and attention is spirit. And at the heart of spirit is mystery. Our need to be in control, our need for mastery, can stifle our sense of mystery, can blind us to the mystery around us.

Rachel Naomi Remen, M.D., is assistant clinical professor at the University of California, San Francisco School of Medicine and author of *Kitchen Table Wisdom*.

54

The Gift of Love

by John Gray

Love has become the Holy Grail of our time. People want more of it, suffer from the lack of it, and search for it all their lives.

For many of us, the difficulty in our relationships is because we have had to adjust to a new way of coupling. In the past, people sought marriage partners primarily to create a family and to ensure security. Now, men and women are more self-sufficient and less dependent on each other for security and survival. Men can raise children, and women can hold jobs. As a result, men and women increasingly seek out each other to fulfill long-denied emotional needs.

Therefore, the basis for marriage has changed. We marry not for survival but for the satisfactions of intimacy.

To attain such love, we must be sensitive to the love we need and know how to get it, as well as how to give the love our partners need. Thus, we must have better forms of communication. We have to articulate those needs as both we and our partners change over time.

Today, men and women have to learn how to negotiate with respect. Men are no longer responsible for simply one area such as the budget, and women another, such as the social schedule. As women earn more of the income needed to raise a family, they want to have more say in how the money is spent. And men want to plan their leisure time. The ascendance of love in relationships also creates a greater capacity for romance and the nurturing of children.

In the past, a sense of caring grew out of loyalty and shared history. Romance was not important or expected to endure. It was considered loving to sacrifice yourself for your partner. Today, people are no longer willing to stay together in a life of sacrifice. If we sacrifice who we are in a relationship, we lose touch with ourselves and our feelings. To us, loving means passion, partnership, romance, and communication. Feelings have become enormously significant. Love, intimacy, and closeness are more important than ever.

To fill my own life with love, I prioritize and carry out the most important acts that create love. In my marriage I've learned it's usually the little things that make a difference. My wife and I have loving rituals. For example, when I'm driving my car with my wife, I always slow down at yellow lights and stop. She's grateful because she knows that when I'm driving alone, I often run yellow lights. Another example is that, even after 10 years of marriage, I still bring home fresh-cut flowers. It's the little things that keep romance alive.

With my children, I make sure that I create plenty of uninterrupted time with them when we're doing fun things. I've taught my children that if they need my full attention when I'm busy, they can always pull on my pant leg. I will stop what I'm doing to listen to them. Also, when I travel, I remember to bring them back something from my trip—a tiny token to make them feel special. The little things that say "I care" are the most effective in filling a life with love.

One way I make sure to get my own emotional needs met is to take time for activities that I enjoy. Even when my wife thinks we need quality time together, if I'm not in the right mood, I take time to be alone—although I assure her that later we can have our time together. When we give to ourselves first, we have more to give to our relationships.

So many people, under the illusion of being nice, sacrifice too much of who they are and thus lose their ability to truly love and get the love they need.

John Gray is an expert in the fields of communication, relationships, and personal growth. He is the author of *Men Are from Mars, Women Are from Venus*. This article was adapted from *The Handbook for the Heart* (Little-Brown) 1-800-759-0190.

55

Care of the Soul

by Thomas Moore

T*he great malady* of today, implicated in all of our troubles, is "loss of soul." When soul is neglected, it doesn't just go away; it appears symptomatically in obsessions, addictions, violence, and loss of meaning. Our temptation is to isolate these symptoms or to try to eradicate them one by one; but the root problem is that we have lost our wisdom about the soul, even our interest in it.

What is Soul?

It is impossible to define precisely what the soul is, but we know intuitively that soul has to do with genuineness and depth, as when we say certain music has soul or a remarkable person is soulful. When you look closely at the image of soulfulness, you see that it is tied to life in all its particulars—good food, satisfying conversation, genuine friends, and experiences that stay in the memory and touch the heart. Soul is revealed in attachment, love, and community, as well as in retreat on behalf of inner communing and intimacy.

Fulfilling work, rewarding relationships, personal power, and relief from stress symptoms are all gifts of the soul. They are elusive in our time because we don't believe in the soul, nor give it place in our hierarchy of values. We have come to know soul only in its complaints: when it stirs, disturbed by neglect and abuse, and causes us to feel its pain.

We live in a time of deep division, when mind is separated from body and spirituality is at odds with materialism. But how do we get out of this split? We can't just "think" ourselves through it, because thinking itself is part of the problem. What we need is a way out of dualistic attitudes. We need a third possibility, and that third is soul.

The emotional complaints of our time include: emptiness, meaninglessness, vague depression, disillusionment about marriage and family relationships, a loss of values, yearning for personal fulfillment, and a hunger for spirituality.

These symptoms reflect a loss of soul and let us know what the soul craves. We yearn excessively for entertainment, power, intimacy, sexual fulfillment, and material things, and we think we can find these things if we discover the right relationship or job, the right church or therapy. But without soul, whatever we find will be unsatisfying, for what we long for is the soul in each of these areas. Lacking that soulfulness, we try to gather these alluring satisfactions to us in great masses, thinking that quantity will make up for lack of quality.

Care of the soul speaks to the longings we feel and to the symptoms that drive us crazy, but it is not a path away from shadow or death. A soulful personality is complicated, multifaceted, and shaped by both pain and pleasure, success and failure. Life lived soulfully is not without its moments of darkness and periods of foolishness. Dropping the salvational fantasy frees us up to the possibility of self-knowledge and self-acceptance, which are the very foundation of soul.

Quest for Happiness

Care of the soul is a different way of regarding daily life and the quest for happiness. The emphasis may not be on problems at all. One person might care for the soul by buying or renting a good piece of land, another by selecting an appropriate school or program of study, another by painting his house or her bedroom. Care of the soul is a continuous process that concerns itself not so much with "fixing" a central flaw as with attending to the small details of everyday life, as well as to major decisions and changes.

So, care of the soul is not primarily a method of problem solving. Its goal is not to make life problem-free, but to give ordinary life the depth and value that come with soulfulness. It has to do with cultivating a richly expressive and meaningful life; it requires imagination from each of us. In therapy we lay our problems at the feet of a professional who is supposedly trained to solve them for us. In care of the soul, we ourselves have both the task and the pleasure of organizing and shaping our lives for the good of the soul.

We care for the soul solely by honoring its expressions, by giving it time and opportunity to reveal itself, and by living life in a way that fosters the depth and quality in which it flourishes. Soul is its own purpose and end.

We know we are well on the way toward soul when we feel attachment to the world and the people around us and when we live as much from the heart as from the head. We know soul is being cared for when our pleasures feel deeper than usual, when we can let go of the need to be free of complexity and confusion, and when compassion takes the place of distrust and fear. Soul is interested in the differences among cultures and individuals, and within ourselves it wants to be expressed in uniqueness, if not in outright eccentricity.

Failure also has a place in my formula for caring for the soul because failure serves as an anecdote for overly high expectations. A lot of the anxiety in life comes from not being able or not being allowed to fail. I understand that failure can be disastrous in the business world, as you climb step-by-step trying to achieve something, to become somebody, to have a position. And yet for many people, failure is an opportunity to take stock of things, to move in a different direction in life, and to reorient one's values. I hear story after story from people who tell me they lost their job—but it was the best thing that ever happened to them. In fact, that happened to me. I was kicked out of a university once, and it was the best thing that every happened to me.

By caring for the soul faithfully, every day, we step out of the way and let our full genius emerge. Soul coalesces into the mysterious philosophers' stone, that rich, solid core of personality the alchemists sought, or it opens into the peacock's tail—a revelation of the soul's colors and a display of its dappled brilliance.

Thomas Moore is the author of *Care of the Soul.*

56

Soul Intention

by Richard Carlson

Stephen Levine asks, "If you had one hour to live and could make only one call, who would it be to, what would you say, and why are you waiting?" A similar question could be asked: Why wait a moment longer to connect with and nourish the soul?

Our connection to our soul is critical to our ability to feel peace and love, to act in kindness toward others, and to feel a sense of gratitude and wonder for life. To nourish the soul means to attend to and care for the parts of ourselves that make us happy and enable us to become kinder, gentler, more compassionate and loving. As we nourish the soul, we move to an entirely different level of life. Many "external" aspects of life that were so important and meaningful will seem insignificant, even silly. Every day, ordinary life will take on new meaning and richness. As we begin to sense the divine in the "ordinary," our "ordinary" lives will become quite extraordinary. Our need to be special and different will diminish, and we will be more easily satisfied and happier.

Is my attention on my external life—what my body looks like, what others think of me, how much money I'm making, how I stack up against others, and so forth—or is my attention on my inner world, the world of the soul? I have often been tempted to focus on my personal ambitions and goals. Over the years, however, I notice that when my attention is on these outer or external aspects of my life, it matters not how well things are going, because deep down inside my being, there is an emptiness.

When I transfer my energy from my external circumstances to my inner knowing, to my "soul energy," my external circumstances usually work out terrifically. In fact, as I parent my children, grow with my wife, write a book, wash dishes, or solve a problem from a place of peace and wisdom rather than one of fear and reaction, my life seems easier, quieter, and more satisfying.

There is something in life more important, more beautiful, and more satisfying than what we "think" is important. That "something" is an internal place beyond thought, beyond form. Our thoughts about what we want, what we wish were different, and where we would rather be will come and go. But behind these thoughts, a deeper level of life is waiting for our attention. This is the realm of the soul.

My inner connection to my soul meaningfully affects what happens in my life. If I'm feeling angry and frustrated, every aspect of my life seems overwhelming and stressful. When I'm feeling contented and peaceful, my life seems to flow. I find that practicing the art of love in my life helps me nourish my soul. Everyday, I find many opportunities to practice love—at work, with my wife and daughters, with a stranger.

An excellent way to practice love is to set your intention on seeing beyond someone's behavior or personality. Try to realize that beneath the surface insecurity, negative thinking, and poor behavior, everyone is connected to God. Just as you wouldn't get angry at someone simply because he or she is in a wheelchair, you need not be angry because a person hasn't yet opened his heart to the nourishment of his soul. When people act in unloving ways, it only means they are out of touch with their souls and aren't feeling spiritually nourished. When that happens, there is no need to panic. The best we can do for ourselves is nourish our own soul by looking beyond the behavior we don't care for, thus practicing the art of love.

We may have more than an hour to live, but why wait a moment longer to connect with our souls and begin practicing love?

Richard Carlson is the author of several books exploring psychology, healing, and spirituality. He maintains a private practice in stress management.

57

Seven Deadly Sins

by Stephen R. Covey

Mahatma Gandhi said seven things will destroy us. Notice that each "sin" is a good thing turned bad because something is missing. Note also that the antidote of each "deadly sin" is an external standard based on natural principles and laws, not on social values.

*1. **Wealth without work.*** This refers to the practice of getting something for nothing—manipulating markets and assets, people and things, so you don't have to work or produce added value. Today, we see entire professions built on the false promise of making wealth without working, making money without paying taxes, benefitting from free government programs without carrying a fair share of the financial burdens, and enjoying all the perks of citizenship and membership without assuming any risk or responsibility.

How many of the fraudulent schemes that make headlines are basically get-rich-quick schemes or speculations promising practitioners, "You don't even have to work for it"? To the degree you move away from the laws of nature, your judgment is adversely affected. You get distorted notions. You start telling rational lies to yourself. You move away from the law of "the farm" toward social and political rules of success.

*2. **Pleasure without conscience.*** The chief query of the immature, greedy, selfish and sensuous person has always been, "What's in it for me? Will this please me? Will it ease me?" Lately, many people seem to want these pleasures without conscience or sense of responsibility, even neglecting spouses and children in the name of doing their thing. But independence is not the most mature state of being—it's only a middle ground on the way to interdependence. To learn to give and take, to live selflessly and to be sensitive, is our challenge. Otherwise, there is no sense of social responsibility or accountability in our pleasurable activities.

The ultimate costs of pleasures without conscience are high as measured in terms of time and money, reputation and relationships. Conscience is essentially the repository of timeless truths and principles—the internal monitor of natural law. "Integrity therapy" is an attempt to align people with their moral conscience—to confess sins, give them up and experience peace.

3. Knowledge without character. As dangerous as a little knowledge is, even more dangerous is much knowledge without a strong, principled character. Purely intellectual development without commensurate internal character development makes as much sense as putting a high-powered sportscar in the hands of a teenager who is high on drugs. And yet all too often in the academic world, that's exactly what we do by not focusing on the character development of young people.

Some people object to "character education" because they say, "Those are just your values." But you can have a common set of values. It is not difficult, for example, to agree that kindness, fairness, dignity, and integrity are worth keeping. So let's start with values that are inarguable and infuse them into our education and training.

4. Commerce (business) without morality (ethics). If we allow economic systems to operate without a moral foundation, we will soon create an amoral if not immoral society. Economic and political systems are ultimately based on a moral foundation. Every business transaction is a moral challenge to see that both parties come out fairly. Fairness in business is the underpinning of our free enterprise system called capitalism. The spirit of the golden rule or of win/win is a spirit of mutual benefit, of fairness for all concerned. One motto of the Rotary Club is, "Is it fair and does it serve the interests of all stakeholders?" That's a moral sense of stewardship toward all who have a stake in the success of the enterprise.

5. Science without humanity. If science becomes all technique and technology, it quickly degenerates into man against humanity. If there's very little understanding of the higher human purposes that the technology is striving to serve, we becomes victims of our own technocracy. If all our scientists do is superimpose technology on the same old problems, nothing basic changes. We may see an evolution, an occasional "revolution" in science, but without humanity, we see precious few real advancements. All the old inequities and injustices are still with us.

*6. **Religion without sacrifice.*** Without sacrifice, we may become active in a church but remain inactive in its gospel. In other words, we go for the social facade of religion and the piety of religious practices. There is no real walking with people or going the second mile or trying to deal with our social problems that may eventually undo our economic system. It takes sacrifice to serve the needs of other people—the sacrifice of our own pride and prejudice, among other things. You can't have a oneness, a unity, without humility. Pride and selfishness will destroy the union between man and god, between man and woman, between man and man, between self and self.

*7. **Politics without principle.*** The focus on the personality ethic leads to the creation of an image that sells well in the social and economic marketplace. So, we see politicians spending millions of dollars to create a superficial image, in order to get votes and gain office. And when it works, it leads to a political system operating independent of the natural laws and self-evident truths that should govern.

The key to a healthy society is to get the social will, the value system, aligned with correct principles. If you get a sick social will behind the political will that is independent of principle, you will have a very sick organization or society with distorted values.

In the movie "The Ten Commandments," Moses says to Pharaoh, "We are to be governed by God's law, not by you." In effect, he's saying, "We will not be governed by a person unless that person embodies the law." In the best societies, natural laws and principles govern—that's the constitution. Even the top people must bow to principle.

Stephen R. Covey is author of *The 7 Habits of Highly Effective People* and *Principle-Centered Leadership* and co-chairman of FranklinCovey.

About the Editor

Ken Shelton is chairman and editor-in-chief of *Executive Excellence* Publishing, publishers of newsletters, magazines, books, audio books, and CD-ROMs on personal and organizational development. The mission of *Executive Excellence* is to "help you find a wiser, better way to live your life and lead your organization."

Since 1984, Ken has served as editor of *Executive Excellence*, the world's leading executive advisory newsletter, and more recently *Personal Excellence*, a digest of the best thinking on personal and professional development. He is the editor of several books, including *Real Success, In Search of Quality*, *A New Paradigm of Leadership*, *Best of Class,* and *Integrity at Work*.

For many years, he has enjoyed a close association with Stephen R. Covey, primarily as a writer and editor on various projects, including *The 7 Habits of Highly Effective People*, *Principle-Centered Leadership*, and *First Things First*. He is a former editor of *Utah Business* and *BYU Today* and a contributing writer to several other magazines.

Ken has a master's degree in mass and organizational communications from Brigham Young University and San Diego State University. In San Diego, California, he worked four years as a marketing communications specialist for General Dynamics Aerospace. He now lives in Provo, Utah, with his wife, Pam, and their three sons.

His book, *Beyond Counterfeit Leadership,* represents a creative synopsis of his writing and teaching, based on 30 years of professional experience, observation, and global travel.

Introducing the
PERSONAL EXCELLENCE PLAN

To help you integrate ideas fron *Personal Excellence* into your life we created the *Personal Excellence Plan*—an achievement and performance program designed to help you find a wiser, better way to live your life, pursue your career, and lead your family, team, or organization.

If you are a subscriber to *Personal Excellence* magazine, you already know the value of powerful ideas to support your personal development. Now, the *Personal Excellence Plan* provides you with a proven system for putting those ideas and principles into action in your life. The growth, improvement, and progress you make will benefit you directly and enable you to better serve others and contribute more meaningfully to organizations and causes.

The plan is your framework and guide, and the magazine will provide action items every month to help you reach goals in the seven dimensions of your life. You will find action items at the end of each article to encourage you to apply the ideas in the article.

What makes the Personal Excellence Plan *so effective?*

The *Personal Excellence Plan* has five unique features.

1. The *Personal Excellence Plan* honors your dreams, aspirations, faith, intuition, feelings, and emotions. *Personal Excellence* is not strictly a "left-brain" analytic, logic-based approach to success. At the start, and at every step along the way, your dreams, aspirations, feelings, intuition, and faith play a vital part in making the plan work. In addition to defining the direction of your life, these creative "right brain" forces serve as visual and emotional sources of truth. They may also serve to suggest changes in direction, speed, priority, or partners.

2. The *Personal Excellence Plan* integrates your personal life with your family and professional contribution. Integrating your personal life mission with your professional development and the missions of the organizations you serve will enable you to make a more meaningful and mutually rewarding contribution in all dimensions of your life.

3. The *Personal Excellence Plan* bridges vision and action. While many achievement programs focus on your vision or mission, results occur only when that vision is translated into action. Through the *Personal Excellence Plan,* you gain access to leadership tools to leverage your time and talent, activate your faith, and make your vision a reality.

4. The *Personal Excellence Plan* enables you to find harmony and synergy among the different roles and dimensions of your life. Often while performing in one role or pursuing one goal, you can enhance another role or relationship or make progress toward another goal, especially if you are aware of potential synergy. So, every time you make a plan or set a goal, look for the double and triple wins.

5. The *Personal Excellence Plan* encourages a balanced, holistic, value-based, principled approach to life. By having you do everything within the context of your life vision and mission, you set goals that reflect your best self and highest beliefs and principles.

The aim of the plan is to enhance every dimension of your life. Use the plan with each issue of *Personal Excellence* to help you reach your goals.